D0126224

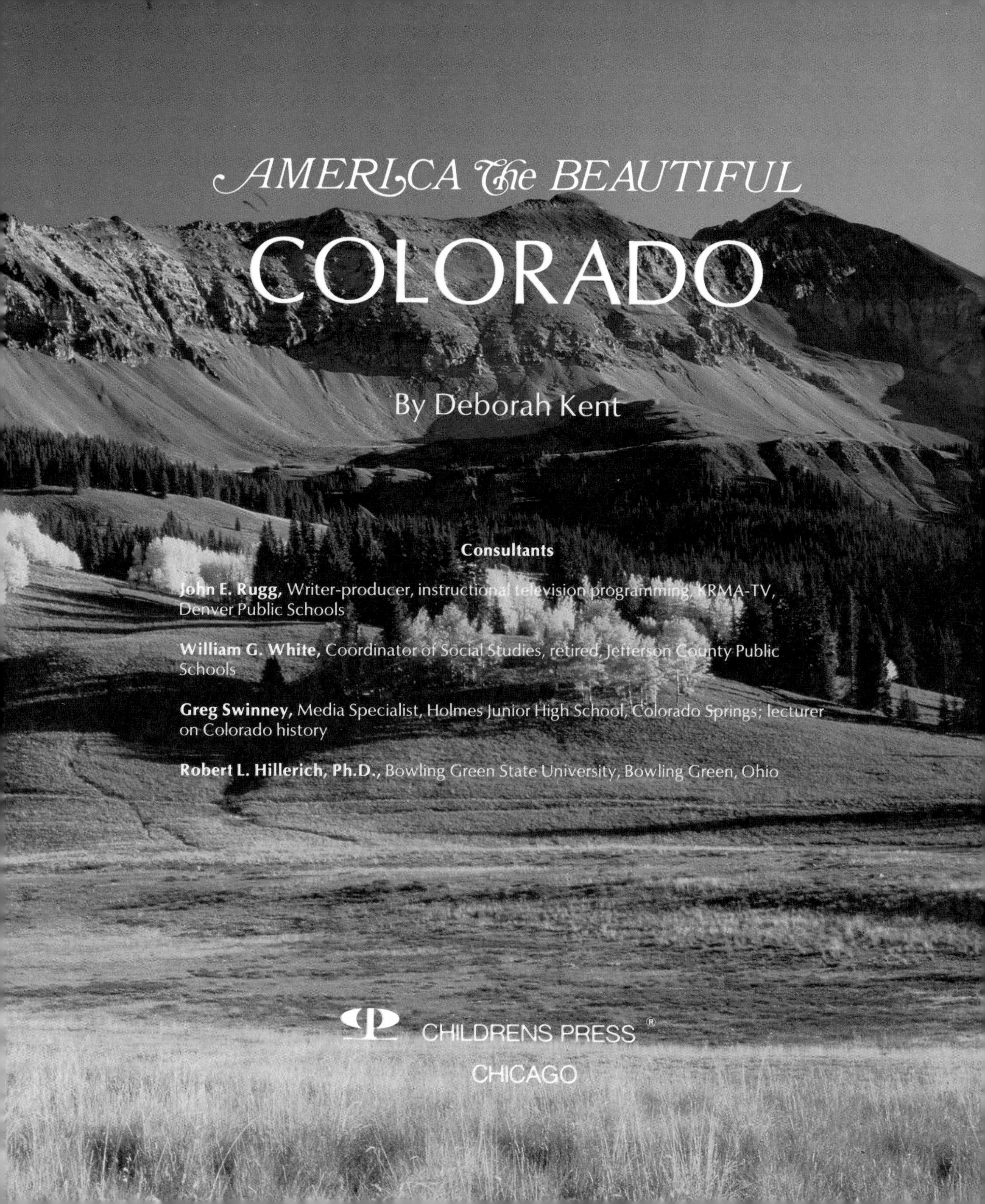

AMERICA the BEAUTIFUL
COLORADO

By Deborah Kent

Consultants

John E. Rugg, Writer-producer, instructional television programming, KRMA-TV, Denver Public Schools

William G. White, Coordinator of Social Studies, retired, Jefferson County Public Schools

Greg Swinney, Media Specialist, Holmes Junior High School, Colorado Springs; lecturer on Colorado history

Robert L. Hillerich, Ph.D., Bowling Green State University, Bowling Green, Ohio

CHILDRENS PRESS ®

CHICAGO

Aspens at Snowmass Canyon in the fall

Project Editor: Joan Downing
Assistant Editor: Shari Joffe
Design Director: Margrit Fiddle
Typesetting: Graphic Connections, Inc.
Engraving: Liberty Photoengraving

Childrens Press®, Chicago
Copyright © 1989 by Regensteiner Publishing Enterprises, Inc.
All rights reserved. Published simultaneously in Canada.
Printed in the United States of America.
1 2 3 4 5 6 7 8 9 10 R 98 97 96 95 94 93 92 91 90 89

Library of Congress Cataloging-in-Publication Data

Kent, Deborah.
    America the beautiful. Colorado / by Deborah Kent.
        p.   cm.
    Includes index.
    Summary: Introduces the fast-growing state of
Colorado, whose dramatic natural beauty lures
thousands of visitors each year.
    ISBN 0-516-00452-2
    1. Colorado—Juvenile literature.   [1. Colorado.]
I. Title.
F776.3.K44   1988   88-11745
978.8—dc19

J978.8
Kent

Aspen is one of Colorado's most popular resorts.

TABLE OF CONTENTS

Chapter 1
I'D RATHER BE IN COLORADO

I'D RATHER BE IN COLORADO

In the mid-1980s, some American cars sported a new bumper sticker. Up and down the highways of the nation it proclaimed, "I'd Rather Be in Colorado!"

Its high, arid plains and nearly impenetrable mountains made Colorado one of the last areas to be developed in the continental United States. But by the early 1800s, Colorado had captured the American imagination. Trappers explored the mountains and valleys in their search for valuable beaver pelts. A few decades later, rumors of gold sent eager adventurers stampeding across the plains. By the end of the nineteenth century, people from all walks of life were making the long pilgrimage to Colorado, lured by promises of cheap farmland and a healthful climate.

Today, Colorado is one of the fastest-growing states in the country. Mountains frosted with "powder" snow draw thousands of skiers every winter. Millions of acres of protected forests and grasslands attract nature lovers. Many of the people who arrive as tourists fall in love with the state's breathtaking scenery and decide to stay permanently. Other newcomers are enticed by jobs in industries that rely on highly advanced technology.

Despite booming resort towns and high-tech businesses, Colorado's frontier spirit is very much alive. For many, Colorado continues to symbolize boundless opportunity—a wide-open land where anything is possible. Every year, thousands of men and women dreaming of fresh beginnings decide that they would rather be in Colorado.

Chapter 2

THE LAND

THE LAND

*Extending as far as the eye can reach lie the great level plains
stretching out in all their verdure and beauty. . . . Then the rugged
rocks all around and the almost endless succession of mountains
and rocks below, the broad blue sky over our heads and seemingly
so very near—all and everything on which the eye can rest fills
the mind with infinitude and sends the soul to God.*
—Julia Archibald Holmes, the first white woman to scale
Pikes Peak

GEOGRAPHY AND TOPOGRAPHY

Colorado's dramatic landscape was formed over millions of
years by battering glaciers, erupting volcanoes, and massive
upheavals in the earth's crust. Several times, the sea swept in and
then ebbed away again. Today, a high, rolling plain covers the
eastern two-fifths of the state. To the west rise abruptly a series of
mountain chains that are all part of the vast range known as the
Rockies.

On a map, Colorado is an almost perfect rectangle. With an area
of 104,091 square miles (269,595 kilometers), it ranks eighth
among the states in size. Utah lies to the west, while New Mexico
and a tip of the Oklahoma panhandle share the southern
boundary. Kansas and Nebraska are Colorado's eastern neighbors.
Nebraska bends to form a portion of the northern border as well,
which it shares with Wyoming. At Colorado's southwestern
corner, the borders of Colorado, Utah, Arizona, and New Mexico

The San Luis Valley is nestled between the Sangre de Christo Mountains (above) and the San Juan Mountains in south-central Colorado.

come together. Known as the "Four Corners," this is the only spot in the nation where four states meet.

Sometimes called the "top of the nation," Colorado has a higher average elevation (6,800 feet/2,073 meters) than any other state. At its lowest point, along the Arkansas River in Prowers County, the land lies 3,350 feet (1,021 meters) above sea level. The highest peak in the state is 14,433-foot (4,399-meter) Mount Elbert in the Sawatch Range. Colorado claims fifty-three "fourteeners"— mountains that stand over 14,000 feet (4,267 meters)—more than can be found in any other state.

The high plains of eastern Colorado are the western edge of the Great Plains that stretch from Canada to Texas. The rippling grasslands of these nearly treeless plains once provided food for millions of bison (buffalo), and later pastured vast herds of Texas

Longs Peak, one of Colorado's "fourteeners," is part of the Front Range of the Rocky Mountains.

longhorn cattle. The grasslands have almost disappeared, and much of the plains region is now irrigated for farming.

Barely fifteen miles (twenty-four kilometers) west of Denver, the Front Range of the Rocky Mountains overpowers the flat plains. The Front Range and the Sangre de Cristo Mountains together form an almost unbroken wall down the middle of the state. In central Colorado, the Arkansas River runs between the Mosquito Range to the east and the Sawatch Mountains to the west. In north-central Colorado, the Park Range runs from the Wyoming border south to the Colorado River. The San Juan Mountains, in southwestern Colorado, are some of the most

The varied landscape of western Colorado includes cultivated fields nestled in mountain parks (top left), such breathtaking rock formations as the Black Canyon of the Gunnison River (top right) and Monument Canyon at Colorado National Monument (above), and snowcapped peaks such as Mount Sopris (right).

ruggedly beautiful peaks in the state. The western fifth of the state is part of the Colorado Plateau, a region of deep valleys and steep, flat-topped hills called mesas (the Spanish word for table).

Between sections of Colorado's mountain ranges lie high, wide valleys called "parks." The largest of these parks is the San Luis Valley, cradled between the Sangre de Cristos and the San Juans in south-central Colorado. Other important parks are North Park, Middle Park, and South Park.

Crystal Creek is one of Colorado's many sparkling streams and rivers.

RIVERS AND LAKES

Colorado straddles the Continental Divide, a crest of lofty mountain peaks that spans North America from Canada to New Mexico. Rivers flowing east of the Continental Divide eventually empty into the Gulf of Mexico or the Atlantic Ocean, while rivers west of the divide find their way to the Pacific Ocean.

Colorado has been called the "mother of rivers." More major rivers have their source in Colorado than in any other state. The Arkansas and South Platte rivers, which are formed in the mountains on the eastern slope of the Continental Divide, are tributaries of the Missouri-Mississippi system that flows to the Gulf of Mexico. From its source in the San Juan Mountains, the Rio Grande crosses the San Luis Valley and flows into New Mexico. Before man-made dams and irrigation projects were created, the rivers on the plains were generally shallow and slow-moving. Writer Mark Twain once said that the South Platte was

Cascade Falls (above) empty into Grand Lake (left), the state's largest natural lake and the starting point of the Colorado River (top left).

"only saved from being impossible to find with the naked eye by its sentinel rank of scattered trees standing on either bank."

The mighty Colorado River originates at Grand Lake on the western slope of the Continental Divide. *Colorado* is a Spanish word meaning "colored red." The river received this name because the silt that it carries colors the water red. The state of Colorado took its name from the river.

The Uncompahgre, Gunnison, San Juan, and Dolores rivers are the major tributaries of the Colorado River within the state. The North Platte rises on the eastern slope of the Continental Divide and flows north into Wyoming.

Most of the hundreds of natural lakes in Colorado lie in the mountains. Many of these sparkling mountain lakes were carved out by ancient glaciers. Grand Lake, covering some 600 acres (243 hectares), is the largest natural lake in the state.

In the mountains, the sun is often so strong that hikers can trek in their shirt-sleeves even when the ground is covered with snow.

In addition to its natural lakes, Colorado has more than nineteen hundred man-made lakes and reservoirs that provide drinking water and water for irrigation. The largest of these is the Blue Mesa Reservoir on the Gunnison River.

CLIMATE

"There is in the Rocky Mountains no gentle spring, no gradual awakening of life," explains Colorado writer James Grafton Rogers. "Summer comes suddenly some day in June on the heels of winter." Through much of the mountain winter, dazzling sunshine glints off fields of snow. At Aspen and other resorts, skiers sometimes race downhill in their shirt-sleeves.

Throughout the year, altitude plays a key role in determining temperature. The average temperature drops 4 degrees Fahrenheit (2.2 degrees Celsius) with every 1,000 feet (305 meters) of elevation. January temperatures at Pueblo, on the plains, average 28 degrees Fahrenheit (minus 2 degrees Celsius), while

A residential
street in Denver
just after a
flash flood

temperatures at Leadville, perched 10,000 feet (3,048 meters) in
the mountains, average 18 degrees Fahrenheit (minus 8 degrees
Celsius). July temperatures average 74 degrees Fahrenheit (23
degrees Celsius) on the plains, but a brisk 55 degrees Fahrenheit
(13 degrees Celsius) at Leadville. Extremes occur in both seasons.
The highest temperature in the state was recorded at Bennett on
July 11, 1888, when the mercury soared to 118 degrees Fahrenheit
(48 degrees Celsius). The temperature plunged to an arctic minus
61 degrees Fahrenheit (minus 52 degrees Celsius) at Maybell in
Moffat County on February 1, 1985.

Precipitation in Colorado averages about 15 inches
(38 centimeters) per year, but varies from as little as 12 inches
(30 centimeters) in eastern Colorado to as much as 400 inches
(1,016 centimeters) in some mountain areas. Major droughts
strike the plains about every twenty-two years. Ironically, flash
floods sometimes wreak havoc in this semi-arid land. On July 31,
1976, 12 inches (30 centimeters) of rain fell within four hours in
the mountains near Loveland. Floodwaters roared through Big
Thompson Canyon, where about 2,500 people were camping for

Irrigation of the high plains

the weekend. More than 135 people were killed and about 1,000 were evacuated by helicopter.

Nature played a cruel trick on the state by granting it plenty of fertile soil on the eastern plains, but sending most of the rainfall to the stony slopes of the western mountains. In order to provide irrigation for crops on the semi-arid plain, Coloradans have created lakes, rerouted rivers, and tunneled beneath mountains in a series of engineering feats that defy the imagination. Even so, the distribution of the state's limited supply of water remains a crucial political and environmental issue.

PLANT AND ANIMAL LIFE

In the 1890s, the last of the herds of wild buffalo that once thundered over the grasslands of eastern Colorado were killed. But the high plains are still home to the pronghorn antelope and the jackrabbit. The lively, sociable rodent known as the prairie dog still lives in some areas. Yellow sunflowers nod in the breeze,

18

Colorado boasts a fascinating array of flora and fauna that includes hundreds of kinds of wildflowers and such animals as prairie dogs, pronghorn antelopes, and mountain goats.

and great creamy-white flowers burst from the dagger-sharp leaves of yucca plants. Tumbleweed, propelled by the wind, spreads its seeds as it rolls over the land. Although few trees occur naturally on the plain, cottonwoods grow along its rivers and streams.

Farther west, on the lower slopes of the mountains, mule deer browse on grasses and lichens. Elk and bighorn sheep leap among the crags at higher elevations. The pika, a rabbitlike rodent that makes its home among the rocks above the timberline, dries heaps of grass to make hay for winter food. The wail of the coyote rings through the state's canyons and valleys.

Yellow pines, Douglas firs, and blue spruces keep the mountain

In the mountainous regions of Colorado, one might spot (clockwise from top left on opposite page) a pika, an elk, a mule deer, a grove of aspens, a stellers jay, or a coyote.

slopes green throughout the year. Just below the timberline, hardy bristlecone pines are gnarled by the constant winds. A favorite tree among Coloradans is the quaking aspen, or "quakie." All it takes is a tiny breeze to cause the broad leaves of the aspen to quiver as if shaken by an unseen hand.

Two national parks, two national grasslands, and twelve national forests preserve thousands of square miles of Colorado land as recreation areas and wildlife refuges. Every year, millions of visitors to these protected regions share the awe felt by Julia Archibald Holmes long ago when she gazed at the panorama of mountains, plains, and endless sky visible from the summit of Pikes Peak.

Chapter 3
THE PEOPLE

THE PEOPLE

"Where are you from?"

This question often arises when two Coloradans meet for the first time, because 58 percent of all Coloradans were born outside the state. Instead of "out-of-staters," some of these immigrants prefer to call themselves "semi-natives," proof of their attachment to their adopted home.

POPULATION

Though it ranks eighth among the states in area, Colorado is only twenty-eighth in population, with 2,889,735 people according to the 1980 census. Colorado has a population density of 28 people per square mile (11 people per square kilometer), compared with 693 people per square mile (268 people per square kilometer) in the heavily industrialized state of Massachusetts.

This does not mean, however, that most people in Colorado live far apart from one another in wide-open spaces. Actually, 81 percent of Colorado's residents are classified as urban dwellers— people who live in cities or suburban areas. Only 19 percent of the state's people live on farms or in small towns.

About four-fifths of Colorado's population is concentrated in a narrow belt of towns and cities that stretches 200 miles (322 kilometers) along the Front Range Corridor from Fort Collins to Pueblo. About half the people in the state live in the metropolitan area of Denver, the state capital. After Denver, Colorado's largest cities are Colorado Springs, Aurora, Lakewood, and Pueblo. Grand Junction is the biggest city west of the Continental Divide.

Between 1970 and 1980, the population of the United States increased 11.45 percent. In Colorado, however, the population jumped 30.8 percent during this period. By the 1980s, Colorado had become the sixth-fastest-growing state in the nation.

WHO ARE THE COLORADANS?

People of Spanish or Mexican descent, usually called Hispanics, comprise Colorado's single-largest ethnic group, making up 10 percent of the population. Most Hispanics live in the southeastern part of the state. About 85 percent of all Coloradans are "Anglos," non-Spanish white people of European ancestry.

Blacks, who make up 3 percent of Colorado's population, live mostly in and around Denver. By 1980, more than thirty thousand Asians were making their homes in Colorado. People of Japanese descent make up the largest Asian group. About three thousand American Indians, or Native Americans, live on two reservations located in the southwestern corner of the state. The Southern Ute Reservation lies wholly within Colorado, while the Ute Mountain Ute Reservation spreads into New Mexico. A large number of people from other Native American groups have moved to Colorado's cities in search of jobs. Native Americans make up about 1 percent of the state's total population.

Nearly 80 percent of all Coloradans belong to one of the Protestant denominations. The Baptist, Methodist, United Church of Christ, and Presbyterian churches have wide followings.

Catholics, however, make up the single-largest Christian group in the state, with nearly half a million members. Jewish synagogues stand in Denver, Boulder, and other cities along the Front Range.

POLITICS

Large corporations and military facilities employ a high percentage of the workers along the Front Range. This densely populated area has traditionally tended to support Republican candidates in state and national elections. Western Colorado, which has many people who are opposed to government regulation of mining and land development, is also strongly Republican. Urban centers such as Denver and Pueblo are largely Democratic. The Hispanic farm workers of the southeast generally vote Democratic, as does the liberal university community surrounding Boulder. Republican presidential candidates have carried the state since 1948.

Yet the only real trend in Colorado politics is the absence of definite trends. Colorado produces steadfast conservatives and idealistic liberals, as well as some leaders who teeter between one camp and the other. Senator Timothy Wirth and Congresswoman Pat Schroeder are harsh critics of the nuclear weapons industry. Elected as a liberal in 1974, Governor Richard D. Lamm grew increasingly concerned that America's economic resources were being stretched beyond their limits. In the mid-1980s, Lamm outraged liberal humanitarians with such comments as "The country can't afford to bring the elderly back to life one day so they can die again the next," and "It's not worthwhile to spend thousands of dollars to teach a retarded child to roll over."

Perhaps the best way to understand Colorado's unique brand of politics is to examine the state's long and colorful history.

Chapter 4
THE FIRST COLORADANS

THE FIRST COLORADANS

According to an ancient legend of the Kiowa Indians, the Great Spirit once planted a tree that reached all the way to heaven. All of the animals of the plain climbed down from its branches to the earth. Last to descend were a Kiowa man and woman, who met the buffalo at the base of the tree. "Here are the buffalo," the Great Spirit told them. "They shall be your food and clothing. But the day you see them perish from off the face of the earth, then know that the end of the Kiowa is near and the sun is set."

For thousands of years, vast herds of buffalo roamed over the Colorado plains, grazing on a lush carpet of range grasses. The herds provided the basis of existence for Indians of many groups. The coming of white settlers, however, at last fulfilled the ancient Kiowa prophecy.

THE CLIFF DWELLERS

Bands of nomadic hunters and gatherers wandered over Colorado's mountains and plains nearly twenty thousand years ago. Heaps of bones and spear points of precisely chipped stone suggest that they hunted buffalo by isolating small groups of animals from the larger herd and stampeding them over cliffs. These early hunters did not plant crops, but rather moved from place to place in an endless search for food.

Mesa Verde National Park preserves such remnants of Colorado's early people as an excavated pit house (above), pottery (top right), and cliff dwellings (left).

Around A.D. 1, a people known to archaeologists as the Basketmakers settled in caves at Mesa Verde in what is now the southwestern corner of the state. Their baskets were so tightly woven that they could carry water. The Basketmakers must have been vigorous traders, for they made jewelry from shells that came from the distant Gulf coast.

By about 750, the people of Mesa Verde had learned to shape bowls from clay, and had moved from caves into carefully constructed "pit houses." The main part of each house was a round pit several feet deep. Above ground level, the walls and roof of the house were built of logs plastered with earth. As the

29

centuries passed, these pit houses were developed into more complex dwellings made of adobe and stone.

By 1100, the early people of southwestern Colorado had entered an era of prosperity that archaeologists call the Classic Pueblo Period. The term *pueblo* is a Spanish word meaning "town." The Mesa Verde people (often referred to as the Anasazi, which means "the Ancient Ones") lived in extensive towns, or pueblos, built into the cliffs. They joined many one-room houses to form great masonry "apartment buildings" that were often three or four stories high. The most remarkable of these cliff dwellings, Cliff Palace, contained some two hundred one-room dwellings.

The Anasazi made exquisite pottery and dammed streams for water storage. They raised corn, squash, beans, and gourds, and traded with distant tribes for salt, turquoise, and cotton. The Anasazi probably lived in peace with their neighbors, for their paintings show no evidence of warfare.

About 1300, for unknown reasons, the Anasazi abandoned their cliff towns. They may have suffered a terrible drought, or may have been driven away by warlike tribes pressing in from the north and west. Whatever the reason, they resettled in present-day New Mexico and Arizona. Their descendants, the Pueblo Indians, never again re-created the spectacular civilization of the Mesa Verde cliff dwellings.

THE COMING OF THE HORSE

In the early 1600s, the Apache people who roamed southeastern Colorado and northeastern New Mexico heard rumors that newcomers had settled in the mountains to the south—pale-skinned strangers who rode on the backs of great, galloping beasts. Soon, daring Apache warriors raided the white settlements

Horses, introduced by the Spaniards, increased the mobility of the Plains Indians, enabling them to hunt migrating herds of buffalo.

of Taos and Santa Fe and captured some of these mysterious animals—horses—for themselves. Other tribes began to trade and raid for horses as well, and began to develop remarkable riding skills. Eventually, the Apaches abandoned Colorado for the deserts to the south, leaving the high plains to the Cheyennes, Arapahoes, Kiowas, and Comanches—all of them master horsemen.

The horse transformed life on the plains. Plots of corn and squash nearly disappeared as the mounted tribes instead pursued migrating herds of buffalo. Families lived in buffalo-hide tepees that could be packed up within minutes whenever the village was ready to move on.

An Indian brave on horseback was a fearsome foe. Artist George Catlin, who lived for several years with the Comanches, described how a warrior could "drop his body upon the side of his horse . . . screening himself from his enemy's weapons as he lies in a horizontal position behind the body of his horse with his heel hanging over the horse's back. . . . In this wonderful condition he will hang while his horse is at the fullest speed . . . [then] rising and throwing his arrows over the horse's back."

A family's wealth was measured by the number of horses it owned, and horse stealing became a fine art. The gift of a horse was a high honor. Horses were sometimes even offered as payment when a man wished to acquire a bride.

One historian described the Indians on horseback as "red knights of the prairie." The horse's speed and grace granted the Indians a freedom of movement they had never enjoyed before. However, the Indians' golden age on the plains was not destined to last forever.

DISPUTED CLAIMS

By the late 1600s, the city of Santa Fe had become the heart of a flourishing Spanish empire that stretched from California to Texas. The Spaniards had two main goals in colonizing the New World. They dreamed of finding priceless gold and jewels, and they hoped to save the souls of the Indians by converting them to Christianity. Although many Indians retreated into the remote mountains and deserts, hundreds were forced to accept the Spaniards' God and to live as virtual slaves.

As early as 1541, Spanish explorer Francisco Vásquez de Coronado may have crossed the southeastern corner of Colorado as he trekked back to Mexico after having explored parts of New Mexico, Texas, Oklahoma, and Kansas in a fruitless search for gold. However, because Coronado's journey was so disappointing, the land north of New Mexico, including Colorado, was ignored by the Spaniards for the next 150 years. Meanwhile, Robert

Cavelier, Sieur de La Salle, claimed the vast Mississippi River system, including the land along the Arkansas River, for the French Crown. He christened the region Louisiana in honor of King Louis XIV.

In the 1690s, a group of Pueblo slaves fled from Santa Fe and found shelter with the Apaches at El Cuartelejo, which was located in eastern Colorado or western Kansas. In 1706, the Spanish governor sent an expedition under Juan de Ulibarri to find the slaves and bring them back. Journeying north across the Sangre de Cristo Mountains, Ulibarri discovered the Arkansas River and finally reached El Cuartelejo. Eager to form an alliance with the Spaniards, the Apaches readily handed over the Pueblo refugees. But Ulibarri was dismayed to see the Apaches using French tools and toting French muskets. Hastily, he named the region south of the Arkansas "San Luis," and claimed the area for King Philip V of Spain.

Although they both claimed the region, neither the French nor the Spanish made any serious attempts to settle Colorado. While treaties made in faraway Europe handed the territory back and forth between the two nations, events were taking place on North America's Atlantic coast that would alter Colorado's history forever. In 1776, thirteen British colonies declared their independence from Great Britain and formed a new nation—the United States of America.

The new American nation was hungry for the vast lands that lay, barely explored, to the west. In 1803, President Thomas Jefferson bought the sprawling Louisiana Territory, which included part of present-day Colorado, from Emperor Napoleon I of France. With the Louisiana Purchase, eastern Colorado north of the Arkansas River and east of the Continental Divide became American territory.

Chapter 5
COLORADO TERRITORY

COLORADO TERRITORY

In southeastern Colorado, there is a river that the Spaniards named *El Río de las Animas Perdidas en Purgatorio*, "River of Souls Lost in Purgatory." The French renamed it the Purgatoire. The Americans, baffled by French pronunciation, dubbed it the Picketwire, a nickname still widely used today.

Colorado is sprinkled with place-names that recall the early Spanish and French claims on the region. In terms of shaping the state's character, however, it was the Yankee immigrants from the eastern states who wielded the most powerful influence of all.

EXPLORERS AND TRADERS

The American people were eager to learn everything they could about the vast new lands that President Jefferson had purchased. In 1806, Jefferson commissioned a twenty-seven-year-old army lieutenant named Zebulon Pike to lead an exploring party into the southwestern portion of the Louisiana Territory. Lieutenant Pike and his men set out from Missouri, collecting specimens of plants, animals, and minerals as they crossed the plains. To the explorers, the grasslands of Kansas and eastern Colorado seemed endless, parched, and barren. They were elated when, after three long months, they reached the snowcapped Rockies and glimpsed the majestic mountain that was to become known as Pikes Peak. The mountain crest lay beneath waist-deep snow, and Pike, dressed in cotton overalls, failed to reach the top.

Lieutenant Zebulon Pike (above) was the first American to sight the mountain that later became known as Pikes Peak (left).

In 1819, a treaty between the United States and Spain established the Arkansas River as the Louisiana Territory's southwestern border. The following year, another American expedition set out to explore portions of the high plains. Led by Major Stephen Long, a party of naturalists and surveyors trudged across the prairie land under the baking summer sun. Long wrote that "[The plain] is almost wholly unfit for cultivation, and of course uninhabitable by a people dependent upon agriculture for their subsistence." For decades to come, Americans mistakenly regarded the area that would one day become Nebraska, Kansas, and Colorado as a desert wasteland.

In 1821, when Mexico finally won its independence from Spain, Spain lost its territory south of the Arkansas River. The southern and western portions of present-day Colorado became Mexican territory. Within a few years, a lively trade developed between

Buffalo robes (above) were among the items prized by the Americans who traded at Bent's Fort (right).

Mexico and the United States. Wagons loaded with American trade goods rumbled into Mexican-ruled New Mexico along the famous Santa Fe Trail, a branch of which crossed the southeastern corner of present-day Colorado.

Among the most valuable items the Americans carried back to Missouri were soft, glossy beaver pelts that could fetch as much as eight dollars in gold. White and Indian trappers searched for beavers through the valleys and mountains as far west as the Colorado River. The Indians traded beaver skins for such American goods as cloth, flour, whiskey, and rifles.

When beaver hats went out of fashion in the 1830s, the traders shifted their attention to buffalo robes. For the first time, Indians began hunting buffalo on a major scale for their hides alone. White and Indian traders brought their buffalo robes to Colorado trading posts, where they were stored before being shipped to Santa Fe and other markets.

Completed in 1833, the trading post known as Bent's Fort stood along the northern branch of the Santa Fe Trail near present-day La Junta. William Bent, the post's founder, was married to the daughter of a Cheyenne chief. He won the respect of the Cheyennes and their allies, the Arapahoes, who flocked to Bent's Fort with valuable buffalo robes to trade. White fur traders, or "mountain men," including Kit Carson, Jim Bridger, and "Uncle" Dick Wootton, also paid frequent visits. Many traders, both white and Indian, brought their families. With wagons coming and going, children playing everywhere, and men and women exchanging tales of their adventures on the trail, life at Bent's Fort was like a year-round festival.

THE HUNGER FOR LAND

Increased contact with the whites brought disaster to the Indians. No natural immunities protected them from smallpox, cholera, and other diseases carried by the whites, and terrible epidemics ravaged their villages. At the same time, the United States government began to pressure the Indians to sell off tracts of their land. William Bent acted as an intermediary, fighting to win fair treatment for the Cheyennes and the other Plains Indians. The Fort Laramie Treaty of 1851 gave the southern Cheyennes and the Arapahoes joint control over a vast territory of unbroken buffalo range between the South Platte and Arkansas rivers. The treaty promised that the land would belong to the Indians "for as long as the grass shall grow and the rivers shall run."

Some Americans were also eyeing the Mexican lands between the Rio Grande and the Arkansas River. In 1846, Mexico and the United States went to war. The Treaty of Guadalupe Hidalgo, signed in 1848, gave the United States most of Mexico's territory west of the Rio Grande, including western and southwestern Colorado. All of present-day Colorado was now American territory. In the following years, many Mexicans moved north

John Charles Frémont (left) led several expeditions through Colorado in the 1840s and 1850s. Rumors of gold drew William Green Russell (right) to the Pikes Peak region in 1858.

from Santa Fe and Taos, New Mexico to farm and raise sheep. They settled in the San Luis Valley, and began building such towns as Garcia, San Luis, and Conejos. These became the first permanent white settlements in what was to become the state of Colorado.

Most Anglos, however, still found Colorado uninviting. Then, in 1848, gold was discovered in California. The following year, thousands of eager "Forty-niners" swarmed west to the California goldfields. To map the best routes over the plains and mountains, John Charles Frémont led five exploring expeditions through Colorado and Wyoming during the 1840s and early 1850s. Mountain man Kit Carson often served as his guide.

PIKES PEAK OR BUST

Through relatives of his Cherokee wife, William Green Russell of Georgia heard exciting rumors that Indians had found gold on the western plains. In the winter of 1858, he set out on an expedition to the Pikes Peak region with a party of Cherokees and gold-seeking men from Georgia. The hardships of the trail forced

After a small amount of gold was discovered near the junction of Cherry Creek and the South Platte River, thousands of ''Fifty-niners'' were lured to Colorado by newspaper accounts and advertisements that exaggerated the amount of gold to be found.

many to turn back, but in July, Russell's party finally found small pockets of the precious metal near the junction of Cherry Creek and the South Platte River, about sixty miles (ninety-seven kilometers) north of Pikes Peak.

Stories of the gold strike flew back across the plains to the eastern cities. Newspaper accounts exaggerated the amounts of gold recovered and the possible fortunes to be made. Enthusiastic guidebooks for gold seekers rolled off the presses. One claimed that gold was ''as common in the Pikes Peak region as the waters of the mountain streams or the sands along their banks.'' Stores in the Midwest could barely meet the demand for tents, shovels, guns, boots, and all of the other supplies necessary to outfit a gold-seeking expedition.

In the spring of 1859, after a man named John Gregory discovered a rich lode of gold ore in the mountains west of early Denver City, ''gold fever'' sent nearly one hundred thousand

One of the thousands of prospectors who flocked to Colorado during the gold-rush era

people heading across Kansas Territory for present-day Colorado. These ''Fifty-niners,'' as they were called, traveled with mule trains, on horseback, or in large, covered wagons hauled by teams of oxen. Some of their wagons bore the painted words PIKES PEAK OR BUST!

Food and water were scarce as the Fifty-niners crossed the plains. Many turned back before they ever reached the Pikes Peak region. Most of those who did reach ''the diggings'' in the Rocky Mountains cursed the authors of the guidebooks, for there was little gold to be found.

''A miner's life is a hard and laborious one,'' wrote Charles M. Clark, a Chicago doctor turned Fifty-niner. ''[He is] cut off from all the comforts of life—cooking meals over an open fire and eating them on a log, and surrounded by dirt and filth that are

Panning, shown here being done in the 1870s (left) and today (above), was the most popular method of searching for gold during the early days of Colorado's first gold rush.

constantly accumulating." Panning was one of the easiest and most widely used methods of searching for gold at these early sites. The gold seeker filled an iron pan with earth and water from a running stream, and shook the contents vigorously to break up the sediment. Any pebbles, including the heavier bits of gold, would sink to the bottom. Swirling off the water and non-usable sand was slow, painstaking work. A man might go for weeks without "seeing color"—catching a joyful glimpse of yellow in his pan.

During the summer of 1859, about $250,000 worth of gold dust and nuggets was taken from Colorado's streambeds. A few gold seekers found the fortunes of their dreams. Others gathered barely enough gold dust to pay for their food. Discouraged, many headed east again before winter closed in. But others stayed on. Some became shopkeepers, some opened saloons, some worked as carpenters. Colorado had become their home.

LIFE ON THE COLORADO FRONTIER

In 1859, Horace Greeley of the *New York Tribune* visited Central City at Gregory Gulch. He found a camp of rowdy miners, living as though they had forgotten the amenities of the life they left behind in "the States." "As yet the entire population of the valley, which cannot number less than four thousand . . . sleeps in tents or under booths of pine boughs," he wrote. ". . . I doubt there is yet a table or chair in these diggings."

But signs of civilization soon began to appear in Colorado. In April 1859, William Newton Byers set up a newspaper office on piles in the middle of Cherry Creek between the rival camps of Auraria and Denver City. There he began to publish Colorado's first newspaper, the *Rocky Mountain News*. Early in the fall, "Professor" O.J. Goldrick (who was said to curse his oxen in Latin) opened the first school in Denver City.

In April 1860, a ceremony on Cherry Creek Bridge merged Denver City and Auraria into the town of Denver, named for James Denver, the governor of Kansas Territory. Denver rapidly became a major supply center for the gold camps in the mountains to the west.

The tents and log cabins of Denver and other camps soon gave way to frame houses. Most towns hastily built at least one church. Shops sprang up, often along a single, unpaved, main street. As the camps began to look like real towns, more men sent for their wives and children.

Gold dust was commonly used as currency, although it had a tendency to scatter. One woman later wrote, "Once a week we would sweep the floor [of the post office] and wash the sweepings, and get quite a little gold dust."

In 1861, the federal government created the territory of

Left: William Byers (back row, right) with
a group of buffalo-hunting friends
Above: Miners standing in front of a lode
mine in the San Juan Mountains region
Below: A wagon train in Denver in the 1860s

A group of Colorado
Volunteers

Colorado by taking parts of the nearby territories of Kansas, Nebraska, Utah, and New Mexico. Though Colorado was not yet eligible for statehood, it now had the right to establish a territorial government that could make and enforce laws. Almost immediately after becoming the first territorial governor, William Gilpin had to deal with the threat of war.

BLOODSHED AND TEARS

In 1861, the United States was torn by a bitter civil war. Governor Gilpin, a man of strong northern, or Unionist, sympathies, feared that the southern Confederacy might invade Colorado. He called for a regiment of Colorado Volunteers, which marched south to join forces with General Edward Canby. The Colorado Volunteers helped secure a Union victory in the 1862 Battle of Glorieta Pass in New Mexico.

Although there was no further danger of a Confederate invasion, tension between Indians and whites in Colorado was rapidly mounting. In 1860, gold had been found on the westernmost fringe of the Cheyenne and Arapaho reservation. Ignoring the Fort Laramie Treaty, which had promised the land to the Indians "for as long as the grass shall grow," the federal government reduced their land to a triangular area between Sand Creek and the Arkansas River.

The older chiefs, who wanted to keep peace, lost control over the younger, vengeful warriors. In 1863, Indian raids on wagon trains closed the Smoky Hill Trail to Denver, as well as the trail up the South Platte River. When a war party murdered a ranching family at Box Elder Creek, not far from Denver, Coloradans feared an attack on the city itself.

In August 1864, Governor John Evans enlisted a regiment of soldiers for one hundred days. Meanwhile, several Cheyenne and Arapaho chiefs opened negotiations for peace before setting up their winter camp at Sand Creek. Most Colorado settlers, however, were no longer interested in peace. The *Rocky Mountain News* called for "a few months of active extermination against the red devils." Colonel John Chivington, a former Methodist preacher, declared, "If any of [the Cheyennes] are caught in your vicinity, kill them, as that is the only way."

On the night of November 28, 1864, Chivington marched his troops from Fort Lyon, and at dawn the next morning they took the camp at Sand Creek totally by surprise. George Bent, the half-Indian son of trader William Bent, was living in the village. He later described the scene of terror and desperation: "The Indians all began running, but they did not know what to do or where to turn. The women and children were screaming and wailing, the men running to their lodges for their arms and shouting advice to one another." One chief, Black Kettle, held up an American flag on a pole as a sign of peace, to no avail.

Chivington later boasted that he and his men had killed at least five hundred Indians. Most estimates place the number closer to two hundred. But all agreed that about two-thirds of the dead were women and children. The soldiers scalped many of their victims and mutilated their bodies. Chivington returned to Denver a hero. The *Rocky Mountain News* proclaimed, "Colorado soldiers have covered themselves with glory!"

When the story reached Washington, D.C., however, Congress called for an investigation. The committee of inquiry condemned Chivington for having "deliberately planned and executed a foul and dastardly massacre."

In 1867, the Arapahoes and Cheyennes agreed to move to Oklahoma. The 1869 Battle of Summit Springs marked an end to the Indian wars in eastern Colorado. The high plains were totally under white control.

THE CENTENNIAL STATE

By 1870, two railroads linked Colorado to the rest of the nation. The Denver Pacific line connected Denver with Cheyenne, Wyoming, a stop on the Transcontinental Railroad that stretched from the Atlantic to the Pacific. Denver was also a stop on the Kansas Pacific line.

The railroads ushered in a colorful era of cattle grazing on Colorado's plains. In the 1860s and 1870s, cattlemen drove their herds north from Texas to graze and fatten them on the lush Colorado and Wyoming grasslands. The cattle were then sold and shipped by rail to markets in the East.

The railroads also brought more and more newcomers to Colorado. Some came to admire the splendid scenery—and simply never went home again. Following doctors' orders, many people with asthma or tuberculosis arrived in search of healing mountain air. Others were lured by dreams of ideal, or utopian, communities, where families would work together for the common good.

The town of Greeley (left) was founded in 1870 by a group of colonists who wanted to establish a utopian community.

The most successful of these utopian communities was the Union Colony. The Union Colony was founded by Nathan C. Meeker, an agriculture columnist for the *New York Tribune*. Greeley, the town established by the Union Colonists, was named in honor of the *Tribune's* editor, Horace Greeley. Greeley, who staunchly promoted Colorado as a land of opportunity, had helped conceive the idea of the colony.

In 1876, Coloradans drew up a constitution and voted overwhelmingly to apply for statehood. Some easterners were indignant. An editorial in one New York newspaper grumbled, "There is something repulsive in the idea that a few handfuls of miners and reckless bushwhackers should have the same representation in the Senate as Pennsylvania, Ohio, and New York." But on August 1, 1876, Colorado became the thirty-eighth state to join the Union. Because it was admitted as the United States celebrated its one-hundredth year of independence, Colorado received the nickname the "Centennial State."

Chapter 6

FROM FRONTIER DAYS TO THE SPACE AGE

FROM FRONTIER DAYS TO THE SPACE AGE

Colorado entered the Union in 1876 as a frontier state—a thin scattering of towns and mining camps. Within a century, it hurtled into the age of satellites and ballistic missiles.

THE LAST FRONTIER

By 1876, the vast herds of buffalo that had once roamed the Colorado plains had almost disappeared. Countless numbers had been slaughtered for their hides. Railroad passengers often fired into the herds from train windows for "sport," leaving the carcasses to rot where they fell. Thousands of buffalo were deliberately killed by whites to destroy the Indians' food supply. As the Indians were gradually relocated onto reservations, farmers planted potatoes and winter wheat on the plains that had once been considered an uninhabitable desert.

Few whites, however, had ventured into the mountains of western Colorado. An 1868 treaty had granted the Ute Indians a vast tract of land on Colorado's Western Slope. But when gold was discovered in the San Juan Mountains, whites began to challenge the Indian claim.

In 1878, Nathan Meeker was placed in charge of a government agency on the Ute reservation. Meeker, who had established the thriving colony at Greeley, hoped to settle the nomadic Utes into a

In the late 1800s, thousands of buffalo were killed for sport by
train passengers who were traveling across the Colorado plains.

similar farming community. At first the Utes tolerated his fences,
classrooms, and threshing machine. But they were outraged when
Meeker ordered them to plow up the racetrack where they
exercised their horses. Many of the Indians left the reservation,
and there were rumors that war parties were being formed.

Frightened, Meeker called for military protection. When troops

Ute chief Ouray was respected by both whites and Indians for his efforts to promote peace between the two groups.

finally reached the agency after being delayed by a Ute attack along the way, they found the murdered and mutilated bodies of Meeker and eleven of his men. Meeker's wife and daughters had been taken captive by the Utes, but were later released.

By the time the troops arrived, the Utes had raised the flag of surrender. But now, the whites were more determined than ever to drive them from their land. "Either [the Utes] or we must go, and we are not going," declared the *Denver Times*. ". . . [the] western empire is an inexorable fact. He who gets in the way of it will be crushed."

In 1880, highly respected Ute chief Ouray and a Ute delegation traveled to Washington, D.C., to negotiate a final treaty. The Utes were allotted a narrow strip of land in southwestern Colorado and small reservations in Utah. Within months, Ouray was dead. He did not live to see his people removed from the land of their ancestors.

After the Ute surrender, Congress opened western Colorado to white settlement. One of the first new towns to appear was Grand Junction, which remains the state's most important urban center west of the Continental Divide. In 1887, British investors created a

The early settlement of western Colorado included the founding of such towns as Durango (above) and Glenwood Springs (right), shown here as they appear today.

resort around the hot mineral waters at Glenwood Springs. Other new communities included Durango, Montrose, and Delta.

Historians define a frontier region as one with fewer than two inhabitants per square mile. With 1.8 people per square mile (.7 people per square kilometer) in 1880, Colorado ranked as one of the nation's last frontiers. By 1890, the population had nearly doubled. Colorado still offered opportunities for discovery and development, but it was no longer a frontier.

Homesteaders on the Colorado plains often collected buffalo chips (buffalo dung) for use as fuel.

MASTERING THE LAND

In 1901, a Denver newspaper ran a story about the achievements of a farmer near Kiowa who "took up a homestead about six years ago with a capital of $1.50 and a family of eight children to support. He now owns his home, is out of debt, and has . . . 18 head of cattle, 5 horses, 11 hogs, and a lot of chickens and ducks." Under the federal Homestead Act of 1862, any adult citizen (or person planning to become a citizen) could farm 160 acres (65 hectares) of government-owned land on the plains. If the farmer worked the land for five years, it belonged to him outright.

Many nineteenth-century Colorado farmers lived in houses made of dried sod.

The promise of such land lured thousands of families to Colorado's high plains in the last decades of the nineteenth century. Gradually, agriculture replaced mining as Colorado's leading industry.

The high plains were covered with a thick layer of sod composed of the dense roots and stems of buffalo grass and grama grass. Because they had to plow up the sod to reach the fertile earth beneath, the plains farmers earned the nickname "sodbusters." Wood was scarce, and the farmers built their homes of bricks made of dried sod. With walls as much as 2 feet (1.6 meters) thick, sod houses were cool in summer and warm in winter.

The farmers planted much of the high plains in wheat and corn. Potatoes became a staple crop around Greeley, and sugar beets flourished in the San Luis Valley. Though the land was wonderfully fertile, it could be cruel to even the most hardworking farmer. Sometimes, vast clouds of grasshoppers descended on his wheatfields, stripping every stalk within a few

The Becker sisters branding cattle on their San Luis Valley ranch in the late 1800s

hours. Some families lost everything to terrible prairie fires. And despite the promoters' slogan "Rain follows the plow," severe droughts occurred every few years. Without water, crops withered and died in the baking sun.

In 1852, Hispanic settlers on the Culebra River began to dig the San Luis People's Ditch, Colorado's oldest irrigation canal in continuous use. In the following years, more and more canals, wells, and reservoirs brought life-giving water to the parched land.

Farmers who lived along rivers, however, often found their water supply depleted as the new canals carried it to more-distant fields. In 1901, the state of Kansas filed a case against Colorado with the United States Supreme Court. Kansas claimed that it had insufficient water because Colorado farmers had diverted the flow of the Arkansas River. The court ruled in favor of Colorado, contending that each state had the right to control the water that flowed within its boundaries. Since the Arkansas rose in Colorado, the Centennial State had the prior claim to its waters.

THE MINING INDUSTRY

The days when a lone prospector might pan a fortune in gold nuggets from a Colorado streambed were long gone. By the 1880s, mining was a full-scale operation, conducted by companies that hired teams of men to tunnel deep into the mountains. Smelters at Denver, Boulder, and Leadville extracted precious metals, especially silver, from tons of raw ore.

In 1891, a gold strike at Cripple Creek proved to be the richest in the state's history. Silver mines made fortunes for investors at Georgetown, Leadville, Creede, and other sites, until the nation's silver market collapsed in 1893.

The discovery of coal deposits in Las Animas, La Plata, Dolores, and Huerfano counties opened the way for new factories in Colorado. With a ready fuel supply, steel manufacturing began near Pueblo in the 1880s. Businessmen such as General William Palmer and John Osgood hoped to make Pueblo the "Pittsburgh of the West."

Colorado's new version of mining offered the average man little hope for improving his lot in life. One Denver editorial declared, "The man who can rise from the wage condition in these days must catch a windfall from his uncle or banks unlocked." Mining companies controlled the lives of miners who lived in "company towns." The most powerful of these companies was the Colorado Fuel and Iron Company (CF&I).

Employees of the CF&I lived in company-owned houses. The company chose the teachers and doctors who worked in its mining towns, and even selected which newspapers would be made available to the miners. Instead of receiving their wages in currency, the miners were often paid in "scrip" that could be used only at company-run stores. Worse still, the company showed

Placer Mining   Cripple Creek - 1893

During the 1890s, Cripple Creek was one of the richest gold camps in the world.

little concern for the safety of the miners. Hundreds of men died each year in cave-ins, fires, and explosions. Company coroners usually blamed these deaths on the miners' carelessness.

In the 1890s, Colorado miners organized to demand higher wages and better working conditions. The Western Federation of Miners eventually merged with the national union the United Mine Workers (UMW). The tension between miners and owners exploded in a series of violent strikes at Cripple Creek, Telluride, and other mining towns. The most notorious of these culminated in an episode that the UMW named the "Ludlow Massacre."

The stage for the Ludlow Massacre was set in the fall of 1913, when the coal miners of southern Colorado went on a massive strike that lasted for more than six months. Forced to leave their company-owned houses, the strikers and their families moved into tents. At last, in April 1914, Colorado governor Elias Ammons called in the National Guard. The soldiers tried to drive some nine hundred men, women, and children from a tent colony at Ludlow Station north of Trinidad. When the strikers resisted,

Residents of the tent colony destroyed in the Ludlow Massacre

the National Guard set the tents ablaze. Two women and eleven children suffocated to death when they took refuge in a cellar beneath their burning tent.

News of the Ludlow Massacre shocked the nation. Ultimately, the public outcry forced John D. Rockefeller, who owned the CF&I, to create a procedure by which CF&I employees could present their grievances. He would not, however, recognize their right to form unions. Major strikes continued to wrack the state for years to come.

Long after the Ludlow Massacre, an idealistic young woman proved that a company could treat its miners fairly and still turn a handsome profit. In 1927, Josephine Roche inherited her father's holdings in the Rocky Mountain Fuel Company. Long sympathetic toward the problems of coal miners, she signed a historic labor contract that promised "to establish industrial justice, substitute reason for violence, integrity and good faith for dishonest practices, and a union of effort for the chaos of present economic warfare." Roche improved working conditions and raised the miners' wages. The miners responded by outstripping every other coal-mining company in the state in production per worker.

YEARS OF DEPRESSION

When the United States plunged into World War I in 1917, Colorado threw itself into the war effort. Farmers rushed to plant more wheat, corn, and sugar beets to meet increased demand. Mines stepped up their production of molybdenum and vanadium, two metals vital in the manufacture of steel. Some forty-three thousand Coloradans enlisted in the armed forces.

After the war, food and mineral prices slumped. A bushel of wheat, which had brought $3.50 in 1918, sold for only 40¢ the following year. Farmers plowed up more and more land, planting bigger crops in a desperate effort to pay their debts.

Battles over water rights continued throughout the 1920s. In 1922, delegates from the seven states along the Colorado River — Colorado, Wyoming, Utah, New Mexico, Nevada, Arizona, and California — met to discuss the use of water from the Colorado River. Overturning the earlier right of "prior claim," the Colorado River Compact, which went into effect in 1929, guaranteed each of the seven states and Mexico a fair portion of the water every year.

In 1929, the economic depression that already gripped Colorado struck the rest of the nation with full force. The struggling miners and farmers of the Centennial State faced even greater hardships in the 1930s. In 1934, a disastrous drought parched the Great Plains. No longer anchored by the roots of wild grasses, the dry, overworked soil swirled up from the fields in choking clouds of dust. America's Great Plains had become the Dust Bowl.

During the depression, the Civilian Conservation Corps provided thousands of Colorado men with jobs in forestry. These men are shown leaving Denver for training at Fort Logan.

In Colorado, the southern plains suffered the most. Around the towns of Lamar, Eads, and Kit Carson, dust clouds blotted out the midday sun. Dust filtered into houses and sifted onto food. Thousands of people abandoned their farms to stand in bread lines in Denver and other cities. Many headed west, hoping to find a better life in California.

Federal programs under President Franklin D. Roosevelt's New Deal helped ease the economic hardship. The Civilian Conservation Corps (CCC) created ten thousand jobs for Colorado men, many of them in the state's national forests. The Farm Security Administration resettled many families from devastated land onto farms near Alamosa, Grand Junction, and Delta. Farmers learned new techniques for cultivation in a dry climate, and planted drought-resistant strains of wheat, corn, barley, and potatoes. Thousands of acres of severely damaged land were replanted with natural grasses.

Tragically, it took another world war to lift Colorado and the nation from the depths of the Great Depression. Once again, farmers rushed to plant larger crops as food prices soared. Much of the land that had been so carefully reclaimed in the 1930s was plowed and planted once more.

More than 138,000 Colorado men and women, one-eighth of the state's total population, joined the armed forces. Many who stayed at home worked in defense factories. At the Denver Arms Plant, 20,000 workers made cartridges and fuses. The Rocky Mountain Arsenal north of Aurora experimented with chemical weapons. Thousands of airmen trained on bases at Aurora, Colorado Springs, Denver, La Junta, and Pueblo. Landlocked Colorado even sprouted a naval air base, Buckley Field. This surge of military activity continued to shape life in Colorado even after the war came to an end.

CHALLENGES FOR THE FUTURE

On August 6, 1945, a ball of fire exploded over the Japanese city of Hiroshima, thrusting the world into the atomic age. The uranium used to create that first atomic bomb had been mined on the Colorado Plateau. After the war, a new breed of prospectors combed the mountains, searching for precious uranium deposits with ticking Geiger counters.

Grand Junction became the center of the state's booming uranium industry. Crushed rock discarded from uranium processing plants was used as landfill beneath the city's homes and schools until the 1960s. When the public recognized the effects of long-term exposure to radioactive material, Grand Junction became the site of a costly clean-up.

Many of the servicemen and servicewomen who came to Colorado during the war returned afterward to make the state their home. Businessmen from "back East" saw Colorado as a land of opportunity. The development of such ski resorts as Aspen, Crested Butte, and Steamboat served as another drawing card. Every year, more newcomers flocked to the Centennial State.

Denver, shown here as it appears today, enjoyed unprecedented growth after World War II.

In 1957, Colorado Springs was chosen as the site of the North American Aerospace Defense Command (NORAD), a vast underground fortress where high-ranking military officials stand ready to monitor and respond to any air attack against the United States. The clear skies above Colorado Springs also made it an ideal location for the United States Air Force Academy, which opened in 1958. In the 1950s and 1960s, Martin Marietta, Hewlett-Packard, Johns Manville, Honeywell, and many other corporations in the computer and aerospace industries opened plants along the Front Range. These industries, relying on advanced technology, brought thousands of highly educated people to the state.

The population continued to mushroom into the 1980s. Growth was most spectacular in Denver and its metropolitan area. Denver became the major center for banking, insurance, and corporate headquarters in the Rocky Mountain states. So many federal agencies have been established in the city that it is sometimes called the nation's western capital.

The quality of Denver's air suffered during the city's unprecedented growth after World War II. Internal combustion engines operate inefficiently at high altitudes. Exhaust fumes from automobiles combine with smoke from factories and wood-burning stoves to form a brown cloud of smog that obscures the city's skyline. In 1986, the Environmental Protection Agency gave Denver the dubious distinction of leading the nation in carbon-monoxide pollution. In response, the city encourages "no-drive" days and tries to limit the burning of wood.

Colorado's growth poses other worrying questions for environmentalists and policymakers. How long can Colorado's water supply meet the demands of the soaring population? Should the state sacrifice wilderness areas to develop vital mineral resources? How can Colorado protect its unspoiled mountains and streams, yet make them accessible to the millions of skiers, campers, and fishing enthusiasts who flock to the state each year?

Some critics argue that Colorado must put the brakes on further development now, before the land, air, and water suffer irreparable harm. Yet to thousands of newcomers, the Centennial State still beckons with a promise of opportunity. As Denver judge Robert Patterson put it in 1987, "The same kind of spirit that brought people west a hundred years ago still survives. . . . Here you're not held back by history."

Chapter 7

GOVERNMENT AND THE ECONOMY

GOVERNMENT AND THE ECONOMY

GOVERNMENT

Colorado's original constitution of 1876 is still in effect, though it has been amended nearly a hundred times. Like the federal government, Colorado's government is divided into three main branches. The legislative branch makes and repeals the laws. The judicial branch, or court system, interprets the laws. The executive branch, or office of the governor, sees that the laws are carried out.

The state legislature, or General Assembly, consists of two houses. The upper house, or senate, seats thirty-five members who are elected to four-year terms. The sixty-five representatives of the lower house serve two-year terms. The General Assembly votes bills into law, and can approve or reject the governor's proposed budget and legislative programs.

The chief justice and six associate justices of the Colorado Supreme Court are initially appointed by the governor. After a justice has served for two years, he or she must be voted into office by the people. The justices appoint judges to the state's twenty-two district courts and to the appellate courts. Each of the state's sixty-three counties has a county court, and the cities and large towns have municipal courts. Denver, whose city and county governments are combined, also has probate and juvenile courts.

The governor and lieutenant governor are elected as a team, and may serve an unlimited number of four-year terms. The governor supervises twenty departments, and appoints most department heads with the approval of the senate.

Three-fourths of Colorado's revenue comes from state taxes on personal income, motor vehicles, and fuel. Highway tolls help to pay for the state's roads. Colorado also has a state sales tax. The rest of the state's revenue comes from federal grants and programs.

EDUCATION

In 1882, Boston's superintendent of schools examined the Colorado school system, which had been in existence for only twenty-three years. He was so favorably impressed that he wrote enthusiastically, "The creation of a system of schools on so large a scale, of such exceptional merit, in so brief a space of time, is a phenomenon to which the history of education affords no parallel." Colorado continues to maintain its high standards in the field of education. All Colorado children between the ages of seven and fifteen must be enrolled in school. In the 1980s, Colorado ranked third among the states in number of high-school graduates.

With twenty-one thousand students, the University of Colorado at Boulder is the state's largest institution of higher learning. The university's laboratories offer unique opportunities for the study of atmospheric conditions and nuclear physics. Other University of Colorado campuses operate at Denver and Colorado Springs.

In all, Colorado has more than thirty publicly and privately funded colleges and universities. Among the state's publicly funded schools are Colorado State University at Fort Collins, University of Northern Colorado at Greeley, Adams State College at Alamosa, Western State College of Colorado at Gunnison,

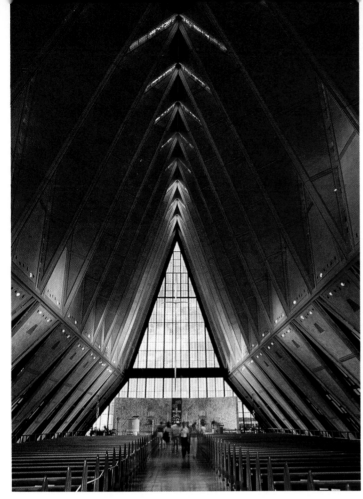

Left: Interior of the chapel at the
United States Air Force Academy
Above: An old schoolhouse in Leadville

University of Southern Colorado at Pueblo, and the Colorado
School of Mines at Golden. Colorado College at Colorado Springs
and the University of Denver are both privately funded. The
United States Air Force Academy is located north of Colorado
Springs.

TRANSPORTATION AND COMMUNICATION

Colorado's mountainous terrain presents unique challenges for
the construction of highways and railroads. The state has 75,000
miles (120,701 kilometers) of roads, about two-thirds of them
paved. The road that climbs to the crest of 14,264-foot (4,348-
meter) Mount Evans near Denver is the highest road in the United

States. Cutting through the mountains at 11,000 feet (3,353 meters), the Eisenhower-Johnson Memorial Tunnel is the nation's highest traffic tunnel.

Denver is the hub of railroad transportation in the Rocky Mountain states. Colorado's 3,500 miles (5,633 kilometers) of railroad track carries passengers to ten cities and hauls freight to many more. The 6.2-mile (10-kilometer) Moffat Tunnel, completed in 1927, is the second-longest railway tunnel in the United States. Colorado is served by twenty-one airlines. Stapleton International Airport in Denver is the largest airport in the state, and the fifth-busiest airport in the country.

Colorado has 130 newspapers, about 30 of them dailies. The oldest and most widely read paper in the state is the *Rocky Mountain News*, published in Denver. Other leading papers include the *Denver Post*, the *Colorado Springs Gazette-Telegraph*, and the *Pueblo Chieftain*.

Colorado's first radio station, KFKA, began broadcasting in Greeley in 1921. The first television station in the state, Denver's KFEL-TV (now KWGN-TV), went on the air in 1952. Today, Colorado has about 165 radio stations and 15 television stations.

THE SERVICE ECONOMY

It has often been said that the United States is shifting from an industrial economy to a service economy. This means that more jobs are opening up in personal, social, and community services than in manufacturing. This trend is clearly visible in Colorado. Such diverse services as banking, insurance, real estate, sales, health care, and education account for 69 percent of Colorado's annual gross state product (GSP). The GSP is the yearly sum of all products and services produced in the state. The largest single

Tourism (above, right) and government
(top right) are two important aspects
of Colorado's economy.

group of people involved in services are state and federal
employees, including military personnel. The Denver Research
Institute at the University of Denver and the Colorado School of
Mines Research Foundation at Golden are among the many
important centers for marketing and scientific research along the
Front Range. The facilities of the University of Colorado and the
National Bureau of Standards draw many firms to Boulder.

Tourism creates thousands of jobs and brings more than $4
billion to the state's economy each year. From October to April or
May, dry, fluffy "powder" snow at Vail, Winter Park, Snowmass,

Aspen, and other resorts lures skiers from all over the world. Every summer, lovers of the outdoors flock to Colorado's parklands to camp, hike, fish, and climb majestic mountain peaks.

MANUFACTURING

With more than forty-five hundred plants and factories, Colorado leads the Rocky Mountain states in manufacturing. Nonelectric machinery, including equipment used in the construction, mining, and farming industries, heads the list of the state's manufactured products. Workers with highly specialized skills produce medical equipment, scientific measuring instruments, and equipment used in the aerospace industry. Other manufactured goods include processed foods, printed materials, luggage, and rubber and plastic products.

Much of Colorado's manufacturing activity is carried out by private corporations that receive contracts from the United States Defense Department. Companies such as Martin Marietta and Johns Manville boost the state's economy by providing jobs for thousands of Coloradans. Many of the state's citizens, however, are concerned about both the ethical issues posed by manufacturing nuclear weapons, and the safety of families living near armament plants. One resident, Jan Pilcher, led a crusade in the mid-1980s to make the public aware of the activities of Rockwell International's Rocky Flats Plant in Broomfield, where twenty-five hundred workers build plutonium "triggers" for the MX missile. "We applaud their very real interest in security, and we don't doubt that it is handled well," Pilcher told a reporter. "But it still makes me shake when I see one of those bomb trucks parked outside the Broomfield Burger King, with part of the crew standing guard while the others grab some fast food."

Large amounts of molybdenum (above) and
natural gas (right) are mined in Colorado.

MINING

The mineral wealth that once beckoned the gold seekers has
helped build Colorado's $2 billion-a-year mining industry.
Mining is carried out in every county in the state. About one-third
of Colorado's mining income is generated by petroleum. Oil wells
operate chiefly in the northeastern part of the state. Natural gas,
found in conjunction with petroleum, is also abundant.

Colorado is rich in oil shale, a type of sedimentary rock
containing a substance that can be processed into oil. According to
some geologists, the oil shale deposits of northwestern Colorado,
which extend into parts of Utah and Wyoming, contain more than
fifty times the proven oil reserves of the United States. Though
shale oil is expensive to process, several companies prepared to
extract it in the early 1980s. When oil prices fell around 1983,
however, the companies abandoned their plans.

Bituminous coal is extracted from both surface and
underground mines in Colorado. Colorado is a leading source of
uranium. Molybdenum and vanadium—both used in the
manufacture of steel—are also mined in the state. Other important

Colorado is a leading producer of sheep.

minerals found in Colorado include tungsten, zinc, lead, and copper. Colorado ranks third in the nation in the production of silver, and fifth in gold output. Though loose gold nuggets are now rare, in the late 1970s a nugget worth $400,000 was found near Silverton.

Colorado quarries produce limestone, sandstone, quartz, clay, sand, gravel, and marble. The marble used in the Lincoln Memorial and the Tomb of the Unknown Soldier was blasted from the mountains of Colorado.

AGRICULTURE

Some twenty-five thousand farms cover about two-thirds of Colorado's total land area. They range in size from small truck farms to sprawling ranches. Although about two-thirds of the state's farm income comes from beef cattle, today few steers graze freely on the high plains. Most Colorado cattle are fattened in feed lots, where, kept in small pens, they are fed a specially enriched diet. Some of the world's largest feed lots are concentrated around

A fall cattle roundup near Crested Butte

Greeley. Dairy cattle, sheep, hogs, and poultry are also raised in the state.

Colorado's cash crops include corn, potatoes, dry beans, lettuce, spinach, and cabbage. Sugar beets grow well in irrigated parts of the San Luis Valley and in the fertile valley of the Colorado River. The raw beets are processed into sugar at plants in Grand Junction, Loveland, Rocky Ford, and other cities. Although it was once one of the state's most important cash crops, the sugar beet has diminished in importance in recent years due to competition with cane-sugar-producing areas of the country.

The most valuable of all of Colorado's crops is winter wheat, grown chiefly on the high plains. To avoid another disaster like the Dust Bowl of the 1930s, today's farmers practice soil-conservation techniques. They plant trees and grasses to prevent wind erosion, and allow some fields to lie unplanted, or fallow, for a year or more to let the soil recover its potential for growing crops. In this way, the farmers try to protect the fragile land even as they reap its yearly rewards.

Chapter 8

ARTS AND RECREATION

ARTS AND RECREATION

Many early Coloradans recognized that they were living on one of America's last frontiers, and tried to capture their vanishing way of life in literature and art. Even today, writers, painters, and composers draw inspiration from Colorado's colorful history, its unique landscape, and the spirit of its people.

The state's mountains and plains invite people—young and old—to pursue recreation of every kind, from fishing and skiing to broncobusting. For sports enthusiasts as well as writers and artists, Colorado is an inspiration.

LITERATURE

The earliest literature to emerge from Colorado took the form of first-person accounts by American explorers. Zebulon Pike's *Arkansas Journal* describes his 1806 journey across the Colorado plain, as well as his adventures with a band of Spanish soldiers who captured him and marched him to Mexico for questioning. Botanist Edwin James, who was part of the 1820 expedition led by Major Stephen Long, published his account of the journey in 1821. In 1841, artist and writer George Catlin completed a massive, richly illustrated work based on his detailed observation of the Kiowas and Comanches.

The discovery of gold in 1858 prompted a deluge of Colorado guidebooks that hid their inaccuracies behind a torrent of enthusiasm. A leading perpetrator of these "guides" was D.C.

Oakes, who lured thousands of dreamers to the almost-barren diggings in the Pikes Peak region.

In his *Colorado: a Summer Trip*, published in 1867, Bayard Taylor wrote emotionally about the dazzling beauty and pure air of the mountains. Taylor's book was read widely and helped establish Colorado as a haven for tourists. Another writer who praised Colorado's scenery was Englishwoman Isabella L. Bird. In *A Lady's Life in the Rocky Mountains*, she described her 1875 visit in which she toured the remote corners of the territory on horseback.

In 1893, Katherine Lee Bates, a literature professor at Wellesley College in Massachusetts, visited Colorado Springs as a summer lecturer at Colorado College. One day she picnicked with a group of friends at the top of Pikes Peak. The panorama of mountains and plains that lay below her seemed to hold the essence of America's character. Her poem "America the Beautiful," later set to music, conveyed her wonder and pride:

> O beautiful, for spacious skies,
> For amber waves of grain,
> For purple mountains majesty
> Above the fruited plain . . .

A new movement toward realism in American literature was underway by the turn of the century. Some writers began to examine the hardships as well as the joys of life in Colorado. Hamlin Garland, best known for his short stories about farmers on the Dakota plains, wrote ten novels set in the Centennial State. Many, such as *The Captain of the Gray Horse Troops*, concern the plight of the Indians. Published in 1923, Hope Williams Sykes' novel *Second Hoeing* vividly depicts the struggles of a German immigrant family toiling in the sugar beet fields of the South Platte Valley.

Though Garland, Sykes, and others revealed the grim side of pioneer life, many Americans still found romance in the days of the Old West. "Western" novels became enormously popular by the 1910s. Dozens of books by such renowned western writers as Zane Grey and William MacLeod Raine turned Colorado's gold miners and cattlemen into larger-than-life characters who were symbols of good or evil.

In a humorous lament for the bygone days of the rough-and-tumble frontier, Colorado poet James Barton Adams wrote a long narrative poem, "The Ruin of Bob-Tail Ben":

> . . . If a man should scoot
> down the final chute,
> That leads to the by and by,
> After leaking his soul through a pistol hole,
> There wasn't no hew and cry,
> But we'd plant him deep for eternal sleep
> In a respectable sort of way,
> And go on a spree to his memory,
> And forget the thing in a day. . .

Hal Borland turned to the lives and legends of Colorado's Indians in many of his books. *When the Legends Die*, published in 1962, depicts the life of a young Ute Indian who is torn between the white man's ways and the traditions of his own people. In *The Editor's Boy*, Borland describes growing up in a remote Colorado town.

Joanne Greenberg of Golden explores the terrain of the mind and spirit in her novels. Published in 1964 under the pseudonym Hannah Green, *I Never Promised You a Rose Garden* depicts the struggles of a teenage girl who spends three years in a psychiatric hospital. *In This Sign* is the story of a deaf couple striving to cope in a hearing world, and *The Far Side of Victory* describes the

A Ute woman etching a design onto a piece of pottery

torment of a young man who causes the deaths of four strangers in an accident on a Colorado highway.

Like Katherine Lee Bates, Ann Zwinger came to Colorado from New England and fell in love with the state's wild beauty. In books such as *The Land Above the Trees* and *Run River Run*, she makes a lyrical plea for the preservation of Colorado's priceless wilderness.

ART

The semi-nomadic Indians of Colorado had little opportunity to create enduring statues or paintings. Yet their colorful beadwork, feathered ceremonial capes, and exquisite jewelry of shells and polished stones reveal their appreciation for objects of artistic beauty.

Like Colorado's early writers, the first white painters to come to the region sought to convey their impressions of the land they explored. Samuel Seymour illustrated Edwin James' account of the Long expedition, and J.M. Stanley painted scenes of Indians and trappers in the 1840s. German-born painter Albert Bierstadt found inspiration in the Colorado mountains when he accompanied a

After visiting Colorado in 1858, German-born artist Albert Bierstadt (above) painted a number of dramatic landscapes of the region, including *Storm in the Rocky Mountains* (right).

surveying party in 1858. Such paintings as *Storm in the Rocky Mountains* and *The Last of the Buffalo* became world famous. Some of Bierstadt's paintings were purchased by European royalty, and one hangs in the United States Capitol.

In the 1870s and 1880s, railroad companies advertised their services with lavishly illustrated brochures enticing potential passengers to view the splendor of the West. Many Colorado artists of the day, including Fitz-Hugh Ludlow and Harvey Young, did some of their finest work for these brochures.

Photographer William H. Jackson, who established a studio in Denver in 1879, brought the West alive with his photographs of the Mesa Verde cliff dwellings, Ute chief Ouray and his people, and perhaps his most famous picture, *Mountain of the Holy Cross*.

In 1871, a patron of the arts named Eliza Greatorex established an artists' colony at Colorado Springs. Lured by the scenery and the incomparable sunlight, hundreds of painters visited Colorado Springs over the following decades. Many made Colorado their permanent home. In 1919, Greatorex founded the Broadmoor Art Academy, which later became the noted Colorado Springs Fine Arts Center.

Left: Baby Doe Tabor shown wearing her
famous ermine opera coat
Above: The Tabor Opera House in Leadville

Even in the 1980s, the theme of Colorado continues to fascinate painters and sculptors. The work of some of Colorado's most outstanding contemporary artists, as well as that of others from throughout the Rocky Mountain states, is on display at the Fine Arts Center in Colorado Springs, the Denver Art Museum, and the Leanin' Tree Museum of Western Art near Boulder. Among the most popular attractions at the Leanin' Tree Museum is Harry Jackson's *The Marshall*, a tribute in bronze to actor John Wayne, whose movies helped keep the Old West alive in America's imagination.

MUSIC

In the summer of 1956, an eager audience packed the Central City Opera House for the world premiere of *The Ballad of Baby Doe*, an opera by Douglas Moore and John La Touche. Considered by some to be America's finest opera, the work is based on the life of Leadville silver magnate H.A.W. Tabor, who scandalized

The Denver Center for the Performing Arts

frontier society when he left his first wife to marry Elizabeth "Baby" Doe. It seems fitting that Tabor's story was made into an opera. In 1879, he donated an elegant, three-story, 850-seat opera house to the town of Leadville. A few years later, he built an even more lavish opera house in Denver.

Today, Denver's patrons of the arts enjoy richly varied programs at the Denver Center for the Performing Arts, a dazzling modern complex of auditoriums and theaters. Boettcher Concert Hall, opened in 1978, is home to the Denver Symphony. The Helen G. Bonfils Theater Complex, housing Denver's repertory theater company, completed the performing arts center in 1980. During the summer, rock, folk, jazz, and symphony concerts are held at the Red Rocks Park amphitheater, located west of Denver. Colorado Springs hosts a noted symphony orchestra and an annual opera festival. The Aspen Music Festival, a summertime extravaganza of chamber music, opera, and orchestral works, has received nationwide acclaim.

Traditional and country music are also very popular in Colorado. A bluegrass festival is held every summer in Telluride, and Cortez hosts the National Old-Time Fiddler Contest. Probably the best-known Colorado performer of popular music is John

Left: A participant in the annual American Downhill World Cup skiing competition in Aspen
Above: White-water rafting on one of Colorado's many rivers

Denver, whose song "Rocky Mountain High" became a theme for the young people who flocked to Colorado in the 1970s and 1980s. Born John Henry Deutschendorf, the singer-songwriter chose the stage name John Denver because of his passion for the Centennial State.

SPORTS

To serious skiers, Colorado means powder. The high altitude and relatively warm winter temperatures combine to produce light, dry, snow of a quality rarely found in other parts of the world. Colorado has more than thirty ski resorts, with slopes for everyone from the beginner to the Olympic contender. Every year, Aspen hosts the American Downhill World Cup skiing competition.

Colorado has 11,000 miles (17,703 kilometers) of trout streams and 2,300 lakes, all of which are open to the public for fishing.

Rodeos have long been popular in Colorado.

Fishermen haul in more than fifteen million rainbow, brown, brook, and cutthroat trout each year. Other game fish include landlocked salmon, silver bass, and black crappie. Black bears, elk, white-tailed and mule deer, pronghorn antelope, bighorn sheep, and mountain goats (introduced to the state in 1948) challenge the hunter.

The rodeo tradition, which dates back to the cowboy days of the 1870s and 1880s, still thrives in Colorado. Rodeos, which feature broncobusting, bull roping, and other events that pit man against beast, are held throughout the state. Two of the largest and most spectacular events are the National Western Stock Show, held in Denver in January; and the annual Greeley Spud Rodeo, part of Greeley's July 4 celebration. The Pro Rodeo Hall of Champions, opened in Colorado Springs in 1979, describes the history of rodeo through photographs and memorabilia.

Colorado is represented in the National Football League by the Denver Broncos.

Professional sports in Colorado are centered in Denver. The National Football League Denver Broncos, who play in Mile High Stadium, became known for having a rugged defensive squad during the late 1970s. Nicknamed the "Orange Crush" because of their orange jerseys, the defense helped lead the team to their first Super Bowl in 1978. Quarterback John Elway was the highlight of the team in the 1980s. In basketball, the Denver Nuggets have given their fans many fine seasons. Center Dan Issel was a longtime powerhouse of that team.

One of the most outstanding athletes to come from Colorado was prizefighter Jack Dempsey, who became the heavyweight champion of the world in 1919. Born in Manassa, Colorado, Dempsey bore the nickname the "Manassa Mauler" throughout his fighting career.

Chapter 9
A BRIEF TOUR OF THE CENTENNIAL STATE

A BRIEF TOUR OF THE CENTENNIAL STATE

"The scenery bankrupts the imagination," commented
President Theodore Roosevelt when he visited Colorado in 1901.
Colorado's stunning natural beauty lures thousands of visitors
each year. Yet the state offers countless other attractions as well,
from the skyscrapers of Denver to the ancient ruins at Mesa Verde
National Park. A brief survey can give only a glimpse into
Colorado's amazing diversity.

THE HIGH PLAINS

The astonishing fertility of Colorado's high plains almost led to
their ruin. Eager to plant crops in the rich soil, industrious
farmers stripped away the thick covering of sod that helped to
hold it in place. During the years sometimes called the "dirty
thirties," the drought-stricken land began to blow away in vast
clouds of dust. Four large tracts of severely damaged land in the
eastern part of the state have been retired from cultivation forever.
Now restored to their original condition, they have been
designated as Comanche National Grassland and Pawnee
National Grassland.
Controlled cattle grazing is permitted in Comanche National
Grassland, but most of the land is protected as a park and wildlife
preserve. Pronghorn antelope bound through the rippling,
shoulder-high grass, and prairie dogs yap at one another in their

A cattle rancher on
the high plains

sprawling "towns." Here the visitor can imagine the days when a
sea of grass rolled from the Rockies to the Mississippi River,
unbroken by highways, railroads, or barbed-wire fences.

Only a few miles from the New Mexico border lies the town of
Trinidad. After the Civil War, Trinidad became the headquarters
of some of the most powerful ranching firms in the West. Coal
replaced cattle as the region's major industry by the 1880s, but
memories of the past survive at the Pioneer Museum in Trinidad's
downtown historic district. Displays tell about the Blooms, the
Thatchers, the Bacas, and other great ranching families. Nearby
Baca House was once the home of wealthy sheep rancher Felipe
Baca, who donated much of his land to the township.

The days of the fur trade on the Santa Fe Trail spring to life at
Bent's Old Fort, east of La Junta. After serving as an important
trade center for many years, the fort was abandoned and
mysteriously destroyed in 1849. However, the adobe structure has
been carefully rebuilt by the National Park Service.

A butte at Pawnee National Grassland

Pueblo, northwest of La Junta, is the largest city in Colorado's southern plains. Established as a steel-manufacturing center by the Colorado Fuel and Iron Company (CF&I) in the 1880s, Pueblo developed into one of the few "smokestack cities" west of the Mississippi River. The steel industry went into a nationwide decline in the 1970s and 1980s, leaving Pueblo with clearer skies but soaring unemployment.

The history of steel production in the region is depicted at El Pueblo Museum. The museum also features a full-scale replica of Fort Pueblo, originally built in 1842. One of the city's chief attractions is the Colorado State Fair. Held each August, it is an extravaganza of rodeos, rides, games of chance, and exhibits ranging from baked goods to livestock.

Among the most striking features of northeastern Colorado are the Pawnee Buttes, two enormous, flat-topped hills that rise dramatically from the level land around them. Nearby, a stately grove of trees stands in sharp contrast to the open plains. Known locally as the Stanley National Forest, the grove actually belongs to the family of Brooks Stanley, a Colorado farmer who devoted his spare time to planting trees for future generations to enjoy.

Greeley, the largest city in northeastern Colorado, has a fascinating history. It was founded as the Union Colony in 1870 by Nathan C. Meeker and a band of followers who zealously believed in abstaining from all alcoholic beverages. Amusements were few in the colony's early days, and there was endless work to be done. One disgusted colonist wrote, "If you can't possibly stay where you are, don't go to Greeley, Colorado Territory! . . . Greeley is a delusion, a snare, a fraud, a cheat, a swindle!" Nevertheless, Greeley prospered. The colonists dug irrigation ditches, opened a school and a library, and fenced marauding cattle out of their cropland. Their neighbors nicknamed them "the saints," and joked that the fence was really meant to keep out hard-drinking rowdies. Unperturbed, the people of Greeley harvested profitable crops year after year.

Today this northeastern Colorado community has become a hub for servicing the surrounding agricultural land. The area is one of the most prosperous farming regions in the West. However, balancing the decline of the sugar-beet industry and the closing of the local sugar-beet factory has been the growth of the Monfort feed lots and meat-packing plant just north of the city. Greeley is well known for its wide streets, conservative politics, the "University up on the hill," and its annual July 4 rodeo celebration.

THE FRONT RANGE

Glistening in the distance, the snowcapped peaks of the Front Range once lured gold-hungry Fifty-niners across the arid plains. Today, the Front Range is the most heavily populated region in Colorado. Nearly 80 percent of all Coloradans live in an ever-widening band of cities and towns stretching for 200 miles (322

**The Tabor Center at
Denver's 16th Street Mall
features more than seventy
shops and restaurants.**

kilometers) from Fort Collins to Pueblo. The concentration of
high-tech industries in the area draws educated people from all
over the nation. The beautiful scenery and easy access to excellent
skiing heighten the area's appeal, and help to make the Front
Range one of the fastest-growing regions in the country.

Where Cherry Creek flows into the South Platte River stands
Denver, the throbbing heart of the Front Range. A brass plate on
the thirteenth step to the State Capitol marks a point precisely
5,280 feet (1,609 meters) above sea level—explaining Denver's
nickname, the "Mile High City." The Capitol dome is covered
with a layer of twenty-four-carat gold, a testament to Denver's
origin as a gold-mining town.

"Denver's destiny is to serve not only Colorado but the entire Rocky Mountain region as doctor, lawyer, merchant, and political chief, as well as banker, butcher, teacher, and supplier of transportation. . . . Denver is much more than the capital of Colorado. It is in a very full sense Colorado's front office." This description, which appeared in the *Saturday Evening Post* in 1946, still holds true today. Denver is one of the youngest and most important of America's major cities. It is the economic and cultural hub of the Rocky Mountain states—an area the size of all of western Europe. No other city between Missouri and California has more hospitals, colleges, banks, and corporate headquarters.

During the city's rapid growth of the 1970s, downtown Denver sprouted a forest of glass-and-steel high-rises. By 1980, as many as twelve hundred energy-related companies had offices in the city. Within the next three years, however, the oil glut on the world market drove many companies into bankruptcy, and hundreds of Denver office buildings posted For Rent signs. Nonetheless, the metropolitan population continues to climb.

Though tensions have sometimes mounted among blacks, whites, Hispanics, and Asians in Denver's neighborhoods, the city has never been torn by rioting in the streets. The Denver area's public schools are among the best of any American metropolitan area, and the educational and economic status of minority groups is steadily rising. Many black professionals claim that Denver offers opportunities that they have found in few other major cities. By the 1980s, a number of blacks served as Denver city officials. In 1983, Federico Pena became Denver's first Hispanic mayor.

A sightseer in Denver can choose among a host of museums and historic sites, and discover endless surprises along the city's streets. Six floors of galleries in the Denver Art Museum feature

Denver's architecture ranges from the beautifully restored Molly Brown House (right) to the modernistic Denver Art Museum (above).

ancient and modern works from Europe, Asia, and North America, as well as an extensive collection of "cowboy art." The Colorado State Museum, within the capitol complex, contains 135,000 artifacts of American Indian and pioneer life and nearly 9 million historical documents. The Colorado School of Mines' Geologic Museum in nearby Golden offers fascinating exhibits on the minerals that played such a crucial role in the state's development. Plants from all over the world flourish at the Denver Botanic Gardens. The Gardens are a fragrant setting for outdoor concerts during the summer months.

One of the city's most popular attractions is Larimer Square, a charming district of Victorian buildings that have been restored and converted into shops, restaurants, and galleries. Sakura Square is a delightful block of Oriental shops surrounded by Japanese gardens. The Molly Brown House is the fully refurbished mansion of the "unsinkable" heiress who survived the Titanic disaster in 1912. The public is invited to tour Denver's United

Leadville, perched high in the mountains of central Colorado, is often called the Cloud City.

States Mint, which helps supply the nation with change by stamping out 22 million coins a day. Denver's mint is the second-largest depository of gold in the country, after Fort Knox.

Satellite cities in Denver's expanding orbit include Aurora; Lakewood; Castle Rock; Golden, home of the nationally renowned Coors Brewery; Longmont; and Boulder, site of the University of Colorado. Each summer, the university hosts the outdoor Colorado Shakespeare Festival, as well as a number of other theater, music, and dance festivals. Ringed by parks, and within an easy drive of fine ski slopes, Boulder is a popular site for conventions and corporate offices. The town's chamber of commerce promotes Boulder as "the closest you can get to Switzerland without changing your money."

The town of Vail lies within an easy drive of Denver for weekend skiing. Created in the early 1960s as a ski resort, Vail resembles an Alpine village. It has been the favorite retreat of such celebrities as astronaut and United States senator John Glenn, Vice-President Walter Mondale, and President Gerald Ford. To the north spreads the Roosevelt National Forest, which is located near the remote Rawah Wilderness.

Perched at 10,152 feet (3,094 meters) in the Sawatch Mountains 100 miles (161 kilometers) southwest of Denver, Leadville is the highest incorporated city in the United States. Snow often blankets the ground on the Fourth of July, and there is a saying that "Leadville has ten months of winter and two months pretty late in the fall." Leadville began as a silver-mining camp, but the area has also yielded rich deposits of lead, zinc, and molybdenum.

In 1878, silver launched the remarkable career of Horace Austin Warner Tabor, whose Matchless Mine was worth millions. Tabor became Colorado's lieutenant governor and financed splendid opera houses in Leadville and Denver. In 1893, when the United States accepted the gold standard, the silver market collapsed. Although Tabor's fortune fell to ruins, he had faith that silver prices would revive. On his deathbed, he told his wife, "Baby" Doe Tabor, to hold onto the Matchless Mine, and she obeyed. Refusing all offers of help, she lived in a cabin beside the mine until she died in poverty in 1935. In Leadville, the Tabor Opera House still stands—a tribute to Tabor's lavish generosity at the height of his wealth and power.

Sixty miles (ninety-seven kilometers) south of Denver stands the legendary mountain known as Pikes Peak. Though Zebulon Pike thought that the peak might never be scaled, more than a million tourists have reached the summit on foot, on horseback, by car, or by riding the famous Pikes Peak Cog Railroad. On New Year's Eve, a spectacular mountaintop fireworks display sets the skies ablaze.

Another natural attraction in the area is the Garden of the Gods, a 700-acre (283-hectare) park studded with immense red sandstone formations. The Utes believed that these rocks were once giants who were turned to stone by the Great Spirit for having invaded Ute territory. Uniquely sculpted by wind and rain, the rocks bear such romantic names as Vulcan's Anvil, the Two Old Maids, and the Three Graces.

The unusual rock formations at the Garden of the Gods create a number of enchanting vistas.

In the shadow of Pikes Peak lies Colorado Springs—or simply "the Springs," as it is called locally. Colorado Springs has a distinctly military flavor. About 25 percent of its population is employed by either NORAD (the North American Aerospace Defense Command operations center) or the United States Air Force Academy. The air force academy, which offers daily tours to the public, is noted for its excellent planetarium and its striking, modernistic all-faith chapel. NORAD is a vast underground fortress that lies 1,200 feet (366 meters) beneath Cheyenne Mountain. Highly sophisticated instruments there track virtually every man-made object in space and are constantly alert for any signs of a missile attack. Other military facilities located in Colorado Springs are Falcon Air Station, Peterson Air Force Base, and Fort Carson.

On the western side of Pikes Peak is Cripple Creek, the site, in 1890, of Colorado's last gold rush. By 1900, Cripple Creek was producing two-thirds of Colorado's gold output and about one-fourth of all the gold mined in the nation. Today, Cripple Creek's famous Melodrama Theater performs at the ornate Imperial Hotel.

THE SANGRE DE CHRISTOS AND THE SAN LUIS VALLEY

To the south and west of Colorado Springs, the Sangre de Cristo Mountains form a rugged barrier between the high plains and the broad San Luis Valley. Early Spanish explorers gave the Sangre de Cristos their name, which means "Blood of Christ," when they saw the striking red hues of the sunset above their peaks. The Sangre de Cristos have seen little commercial development, though Westcliffe is gaining popularity as a ski resort. One of the region's most amazing sights is the Great Sand Dunes National

**Great Sand Dunes
National Monument**

Monument, an otherworldly landscape of shifting dunes that
sometimes stand as high as 1,200 feet (366 meters).

Beyond the Sangre de Cristos lies the high, wide valley of the
Rio Grande, known as the San Luis Valley. During the 1850s, the
area was settled by farmers and ranchers from Mexico. Hispanic
influence is still strong in the region. In the 1890s, when sugar
beet farming began to take hold in Colorado's valleys, many
German-Russian sugar-beet farmers brought their expertise to the
Sun Luis Valley. Today, the valley's irrigation system enables
farmers to raise potatoes, lettuce, cabbage, spinach, and carrots.

About twenty-five miles (forty kilometers) east of Alamosa
stands Fort Garland, established in 1858 to protect settlers in the
valley. In 1866, during a period of tension between whites and
Indians, Kit Carson commanded a unit of federal troops there. The
fort served as an army post until 1883. Visitors can view exhibits
on military life of the period and explore the commandant's
quarters, which are restored to look as they did during Kit
Carson's time.

Partially unearthed dinosaur
bones and fossils (above)
are on display at Dinosaur
National Monument (right).

THE WESTERN SLOPE

The ridge of mountain crests known as the Continental Divide
snakes to the southwest across Colorado from Rocky Mountain
National Park in the north to Archuleta County on the New
Mexico border. The immense terrain of mountains and plateaus
west of the divide is known to Coloradans as the Western Slope.
Most of Colorado's 14 million acres (5.7 million hectares) of
national forestland are on the Western Slope, where the
population is sparse and the frontier spirit is still very much alive.

Northwestern Colorado is oil shale country—the land of the
rocks that burn. When heated to 900 degrees Fahrenheit (500
degrees Celsius), oil shale yields a viscous black substance called
shale oil. The process is costly, and so far, Colorado's vast shale-
oil reserves have scarcely been tapped.

One of the most exciting ways to explore the remote canyons of
the Green and Yampa rivers of the Colorado Plateau is by raft.
Rafts can dodge the rocks at hairpin bends and sweep over
breathtaking falls. Some adventurers challenge the rivers in tiny,

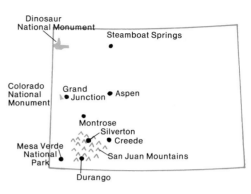

An outdoor cafe in Aspen

inflatable two-man rafts, while others prefer a guided tour, complete with meals.

In Colorado's northwestern corner, Dinosaur National Monument straddles the Utah border. Dinosaur buffs can marvel at the bones and footprints of fourteen species that have been unearthed in the vicinity. Amateur fossil hunters enjoy searching the canyons for traces of the ancient reptiles.

One of the many busy ski resorts on the Western Slope is Steamboat Springs. To pioneers, the spring that still bubbles in the town's main park sounded like a steamboat whistle. Steamboat Springs is surrounded by ranching country. A sign in the window of one downtown shop proclaims: "We outfit the family and the horse."

In 1947, Chicago businessman Joseph Pepcke saw potential in the decaying mining town of Aspen, and began transforming it into one of the most glamorous resorts in Colorado. In addition to

A winter fireworks display over Aspen Mountain

building ski runs for winter visitors, Pepcke founded the Aspen
Institute for Humanistic Studies, where some of the nation's top
political and intellectual leaders gather every summer to share
ideas. ''Thinking is to summer in Colorado what skiing is to
winter,'' said Collins Williams, the institute's director, in 1986.
''When the snow melts from the high country . . . the mountains
become a natural refuge for the nation's harried power brokers.''
Arms control, energy, and the environment are among the
complex topics discussed at the Aspen Institute and at similar
''think tanks'' in Telluride, Denver, and Vail.

Arms-control and energy issues have a direct bearing on the
lives of the people of Grand Junction in the heart of Colorado's
uranium belt. In the early 1980s, uranium prices plunged from

Maroon Bells near Aspen are among Colorado's most-photographed peaks.

forty-three dollars to twenty dollars a pound, and many miners lost their jobs. Some resent the private citizens and public officials who question the safety of nuclear generators. "We're out of the market because of the bad judgment of the hippie class," one miner told a reporter. "People who oppose nuclear power don't know what they're saying."

Directly west of Grand Junction is Colorado National Monument. Established in 1911, the monument is a wildlife preserve encompassing 18,000 acres (7,284 hectares). Devil's Kitchen, Window Rock, and Monolith Parade are among the exotic rock formations that can be seen there.

The Durango and Silverton Narrow Gauge Railroad (left), built originally to haul silver out of the mines, now takes tourists on excursions between the old mining towns of Durango and Silverton (above).

Four miles (six kilometers) south of Montrose is the Ute Indian Museum. Considered one of Colorado's best museums, it features exhibits that reveal many aspects of Ute life and beliefs. It also commemorates the life of Chief Ouray, the great peacemaker and leader of the Ute Indians and the most famous Indian in Colorado history. The grave of Ouray's wife, Chipeta, is on the museum grounds.

The San Juan Mountains in southwestern Colorado furnish some of the state's most ruggedly beautiful scenery. In December 1873, a sudden blizzard in the San Juan Range doomed the gold-seeking party of Alferd E. Packer. Packer was the only one to survive the ordeal, and he was later convicted of murdering and cannibalizing his five companions. Over the years, Packer's story became a legend, and sometimes even sparked macabre humor. In 1986, students at the University of Colorado in Boulder voted to name one of their dining halls the Alferd E. Packer Memorial Grill.

To negotiate the steep inclines and tortuous turns of Colorado's mountains, early railroad builders used special "narrow-gauge" tracks that were set closer together than standard tracks. One of the last narrow-gauge railroads still in operation runs year-round between Durango and Silverton.

The sleepy village of Creede bears few traces of its brief era as a silver boomtown. After Nicholas Creede discovered silver at Willow Creek in 1889, as many as three hundred silver hunters a day flocked to the town. Until the silver crisis of 1893, Creede was an endless carnival of dance halls, saloons, and overnight fortunes. Poet Cy Warman immortalized those glorious days:

> It's day all day in the day-time,
> and there is no night in Creede.

Not far from the spot where the corners of Colorado, Utah, Arizona, and New Mexico all meet, Mesa Verde National Park preserves architectural remnants of the Anasazi, Colorado's earliest settled inhabitants. Their terraced dwellings, carved into sandstone cliffs, are not unlike apartment buildings of today. The large cylindrical chambers, or *kivas*, at the base of these structures were used for ceremonial and religious purposes. Every year, as many as six hundred thousand visitors marvel at the sophisticated Anasazi architecture and wonder about this mysterious civilization that rose and vanished amid these rugged mountains.

"To write of such a wonderland can only be a labor of love for those to whom its rare beauty has been revealed," wrote Colorado historian Frank Hall in 1869. For millions of visitors, for eager newcomers who flocked to its cities, and for those who have lived there all their lives, Colorado is still a land of wonders.

FACTS AT A GLANCE

GENERAL INFORMATION

Statehood: August 1, 1876, thirty-eighth state

Origin of Name: Named for the Colorado River; early Spanish explorers called the river *Colorado* (colored red) because the silt carried by the river colored it red.

State Capital: Denver, founded 1858

State Nickname: "Centennial State"

State Flag: Colorado's state flag was adopted in 1911. Three equal horizontal bands—blue, white, and blue—symbolize the state's blue skies and mountain snows. In the center, a red "c," representing Colorado, is curved around a yellow ball that symbolizes gold's importance in the state.

State Motto: *Nil sine Numine,* "Nothing Without Providence"

State Bird: Lark bunting

State Animal: Rocky Mountain sheep (bighorn)

State Flower: Rocky Mountain columbine

State Tree: Colorado blue spruce

State Gem: Aquamarine

State Song: "Where the Columbines Grow," words and music by A.J. Fynn, adopted as the state song in 1915:

> Where the snowy peaks gleam in the moonlight,
> Above the dark forests of pine,
> And the wild foaming waters dash onward
> Toward lands where the tropic stars shine;
>
> Where the scream of the bold mountain eagle,
> Responds to the notes of the dove,
> Is the purple robed West, the land that is best,
> The pioneer land that we love.

Camping in the Rockies

Chorus:
'Tis the land where the columbines grow,
Over-looking the plains far below,
While the cool summer breeze in the evergreen trees
Softly sings where the columbines grow.

The bison is gone from the upland,
The deer from the canyon has fled,
The home of the wolf is deserted,
The antelope moans for his dead,

The war whoop re-echoes no longer
The Indian's only a name,
And the nymphs of the grove in their loneliness rove,
But the columbine blooms just the same.

(Chorus)

Let the violet brighten the brookside,
In sunlight of earlier spring,
Let the clover bedeck the green meadow,
In days when the orioles sing,

Let the goldenrod herald the autumn,
But under the midsummer sky,
In its fair Western home, may the columbine bloom
Till our great mountain rivers run dry.

(Chorus)

POPULATION

Population: 2,889,735, twenty-eighth among the states (1980 census)

Population Density: 28 persons per sq. mi. (11 persons per km²)

Population Distribution: 81 percent of the people live in cities or towns. Denver, the state capital, is Colorado's largest city.

Denver	492,365
Colorado Springs	214,821
Aurora	158,588
Lakewood	113,808
Pueblo	101,686
Arvada	84,576
Boulder	76,685
Fort Collins	65,092
Greeley	53,006

(Population figures according to 1980 census)

Population Growth: Colorado's rapid population growth has been tied closely to the state's economy. The discovery of gold near Denver in 1858 ushered in a mining era that saw a fivefold population increase by 1880. Agriculture superceded mining as the mainstay of the state's economy in the early 1900s, bringing a new wave of immigrants. During World War II, when Colorado became a center for defense facilities and a source of minerals used in war materials, another new wave of workers came to the state. Since the war, Colorado has been one of the nation's fastest-growing states. From 1970 to 1980, the state's population grew an astounding 30.8 percent, while the population of the entire nation grew 11.45 percent. The list below shows population growth in Colorado since 1870:

Year	Population
1870	39,864
1880	194,327
1900	539,700
1920	939,629
1940	1,123,296
1950	1,325,089
1960	1,753,947
1970	2,209,596
1980	2,889,735

GEOGRAPHY

Borders: States that border Colorado are Wyoming and Nebraska on the north, Nebraska and Kansas on the east, Oklahoma and New Mexico on the south, Arizona at the southwest corner, and Utah on the west.

Rafters on the Arkansas River

Highest Point: Mount Elbert, 14,433 ft. (4,399 m)

Lowest Point: Along the Arkansas River at the Colorado-Kansas border, 3,350 ft (1,021 m)

Greatest Distances: North to south—275 mi. (442 km)
East to west—385 mi. (620 km)

Area: 104,091 sq. mi. (269,595 km²)

Rank in Area Among the States: Eighth

National Forests and Parklands: Colorado has twelve national forests occupying some 13.8 million acres (5.6 million hectares) of land. Arapaho, Grand Mesa, Gunnison, Pike, Rio Grande, Roosevelt, Routt, San Isabel, San Juan, Uncompahgre, and White River national forests lie completely within the state; Manti-La Sal National Forest lies in both Colorado and Utah. Colorado also has two national parks, Rocky Mountain and Mesa Verde, and seven national monuments. In all, the United States government owns about one-third of the state.

Rivers: The Colorado River is the largest river west of the Rocky Mountains. It drains about one-twelfth of the entire United States and is the principal water source for western Colorado and much of the southwestern United States. The Colorado begins at Grand Lake on the west slope of the Front Range and flows southwest across the state. Its principal tributaries in Colorado include the Uncompahgre, Gunnison, San Juan, Dolores, Animas, Blue, Piedra, White, and Yampa rivers. Three major Colorado rivers east of the Continental Divide are the Arkansas, the Republican, and the South Platte. Other major rivers that begin in Colorado are the Rio Grande, which rises in the San Juan Mountains; and the

112

Uncompahgre National Forest

North Platte, which rises in North Park. As Colorado's rivers rush down the steep slopes of the Rockies, they have created beautiful falls, gorges, and canyons, including the Royal Gorge of the Arkansas River and the spectacular Black Canyon of the Gunnison.

Lakes: Colorado's largest lake is man-made Blue Mesa Reservoir on the Gunnison River. The state has more than 1,900 artificial lakes that have been created by damming some of its many rivers and streams. Nearly thirty diversion projects cut over and through the mountains to deliver water to the drier, and most heavily populated, eastern slopes. Colorado's largest natural lake, covering 600 acres (243 hectares), is glacier-formed Grand Lake on the west slope of the Front Range. Summit Lake, which lies 12,740 ft. (3,883 m) above sea level, is one of the nation's highest lakes. Hundreds of small, natural lakes can be found in the mountains. The state also has eighteen active hot springs. Great Pagosa Springs in Archuleta County is the largest.

Topography: Five hundred million years ago, Colorado was a vast, level plain. Today, it has the highest average elevation (6,800 ft./2,073 m) of any state in the nation. About a thousand Colorado peaks rise higher than 10,000 ft. (3,048 m), and more than fifty peaks tower over the 14,000-ft. (4,267-m) mark. During its geological history, the state has been submerged beneath an ancient sea at least four times, ripped open as mountains heaved up, scoured by glaciers, fired by volcanoes, and eroded by wind and water. The resulting landscape is divided into four main topographic regions: the Great Plains, the Rocky Mountains, the Colorado Plateau, and the Intermontane (or Wyoming) Basin.

The Great Plains occupy the eastern two-fifths of the state. From an elevation of about 3,500 ft. (1,067 m) at the Kansas-Nebraska border, the region gradually climbs westward to about 5,000 ft. (1,524 m) at the base of the foothills. The South Platte and Arkansas rivers cut through the generally treeless and level Great Plains. Large-scale agriculture, common in the region, depends on irrigation in the valleys or dry farming in the higher elevations.

Colorado's mountainous regions receive heavy winter snowfall.

The Rocky Mountains occupy the central two-fifths of the state. The Continental Divide, the main watershed of the continent, runs from north to south through the Rockies. Streams west of the Continental Divide flow eventually into the Pacific Ocean; streams east of it flow eventually into the Atlantic Ocean. The divide separates the Western and Eastern slopes of the Rocky Mountains. The major ranges of the Western Slope are the Park Range, the Sawatch Range, and the San Juan Mountains. The Sawatch is Colorado's highest range; it contains Colorado's highest peak, Mount Elbert (14,433 ft./4,399 m). On the east, the Front Range and the Sangre de Cristo Mountains wall off the Rockies from the Great Plains region. Pikes Peak (14,110 ft./4,301 m), Longs Peak (14,255 ft./4,345 m), and Mount Evans (14,264 ft./4,348 m) are part of the Front Range. The eastern foothills, known as the Colorado Piedmont, boast four-fifths of the state's population, its largest cities, and most of its major industries and universities. Between the ranges of the Colorado Rockies are high-altitude valleys or basins called "parks." The largest park is the San Juan Valley, in south-central Colorado. Covering an area nearly the size of Connecticut, it is surrounded by the Sangre de Cristo and San Juan mountains. North Park, Middle Park, and South Park are other large mountain parks.

The Colorado Plateau covers most of the remaining fifth of the state. It is a mostly arid region of broad, flat plateaus slashed by deep ravines and gorges and dotted with high, flat-topped mesas. In the northwest corner of the state lies the small region of rolling hills and plateaus known as the Intermontane or Wyoming Basin. Cattle and sheep graze the Colorado Plateau and Intermontane Basin regions.

Climate: Colorado's climate is generally sunny and dry. However, weather conditions may vary greatly within relatively short distances according to changes in altitude. The high mountains see cool summers and cold, snowy winters. Deep layers of snow may remain year-round on the highest peaks. January temperatures average 18° F. (-8° C) in Leadville in the mountains and 28° F. (-2° C) in Burlington on the plains. July temperatures average 55° F. (13° C) at Leadville and 74° F.

(23° C) at Burlington. Colorado's lowest recorded temperature was -61° F. (-52° C) at Maybell, in the state's northwest corner, on February 1, 1985. The state's highest recorded temperature was 118° F. (48° C) at Bennett, east of Denver, on July 11, 1888. The chinook, a warm, dry wind that blows down the eastern slopes in the winter, may raise temperatures 30-40° F. (16-22° C) in less than an hour and create violent, sudden winds of over 100 mi. (161 km) per hour. Annual precipitation (rain and snow) in the state averages about 15 in. (38 cm), but varies greatly from region to region. In the Rockies, as much as 400 in. (1,016 cm) of snow may accumulate yearly, with Denver averaging 59 in. (150 cm). In contrast, the San Luis Valley ranges from a low of 7 in. (18 cm) to a high of 27 in. (69 cm) of total precipitation.

NATURE

Trees: Ashes, aspens, cottonwoods, Douglas and other firs, junipers, maples, oaks, piñon and ponderosa pines, blue and Engelmann spruces

Wild Plants: Anemones, buttercups, columbines, daisies, forget-me-nots, gentians, wild geraniums, wild irises, larkspurs, mountain lilies, mosses and lichens, orchids, Indian paintbrushes, pasqueflowers, prickly poppies, wild roses, sagebrush, greasewood, sedges, shooting stars, violets, yarrows, yucca, many varieties of grasses and cacti

Animals: Antelope, elk, black bears, beavers, bobcats, foxes, jackrabbits, pikas, coyotes, mountain goats, mountain lions, marmots, martens, mule deer, prairie dogs, rabbits, Rocky Mountain sheep (bighorns), skunks

Birds: Bluebirds, lark buntings, chickadees, prairie chickens, mourning doves, ducks, grouse, blue jays, Rocky Mountain jays, meadowlarks, orioles, pheasants, quail, sparrows, thrashers, thrushes

Fish: Bass, bluegills, bullheads, catfish, crappies, perch, salmon, trout

GOVERNMENT

The government of Colorado, like the federal government, is divided into three branches—legislative, executive, and judicial. The state's legislative branch, called the General Assembly, is made up of a senate with thirty-five members and a house of representatives with sixty-five members. Members of the senate are elected to four-year terms; members of the house of representatives serve two-year terms. The General Assembly votes bills into law and determines how state revenue will be spent.

The executive branch, headed by the governor, administers the law. The governor is elected to a four-year term and may serve an unlimited number of terms. The state constitution gives the governor power to veto legislation, grant pardons, and serve as commander-in-chief of the state militia. The governor has the power to appoint most of the heads of state departments.

Guggenheim Hall at the Colorado School of Mines at Golden

The judicial branch interprets the law and tries cases. The state's highest court, the supreme court, consists of a chief justice and six associate justices. Members of the supreme court are initially appointed by the governor, but after serving two years, they must be elected to office by the people. If elected, they then serve ten-year terms. The second-highest court in Colorado is the six-member court of appeals. Appellate judges are initially appointed, then elected to eight-year terms. The lowest courts, where most cases are heard, are the twenty-two district courts. District court judges are initially appointed by the governor, then elected to six-year terms. Each of the state's sixty-three counties has a county court, and the larger towns have municipal courts. Denver also has probate and juvenile courts.

Number of Counties: 63

U.S. Representatives: 6

Electoral Votes: 8

Voting Qualifications: Eighteen years of age, one-year residency in the state, ninety days in the county, and twenty days in the district

EDUCATION

About 540,000 children are enrolled in Colorado public schools, at an average cost of $3,171 per pupil. Another 33,000 students are enrolled in private schools. Public-school education is controlled by a state board of education whose members are elected from each of the state's congressional districts. There are 176 local school districts.

Colorado has more than thirty institutions of higher learning. The University of Colorado, with its main campus at Boulder and campuses at Colorado Springs and

Denver, is the state's largest university. Total enrollment is approximately 49,000 students. Another 18,000 students are enrolled at Colorado State University at Fort Collins. Other state-supported colleges include the internationally known Colorado School of Mines at Golden, University of Northern Colorado at Greeley, Adams State College at Alamosa, Western State College of Colorado at Gunnison, University of Southern Colorado at Pueblo, Fort Lewis College at Durango, Colorado Technical College at Colorado Springs, and Metropolitan State College at Denver. The United States Air Force Academy, one of the nation's service academies, is located near Colorado Springs. Private colleges include the University of Denver, Loretto Heights College, and Regis College, all in Denver; and Colorado College in Colorado Springs. Community colleges are located in Colorado Springs, Glenwood Springs, Grand Junction, La Junta, Lamar, Leadville, Littleton, Rangeley, Sterling, and Trinidad.

ECONOMY AND INDUSTRY

Principal Products:
Agriculture: Beef cattle, sheep, wheat, corn, hay, dairy products, alfalfa, cabbage, cantaloupes, dry beans, lettuce, onions, potatoes, spinach, tomatoes, apples, cherries, peaches, pears, flowers and greenhouse products

Manufacturing: Nonelectrical machinery, chemical and allied products, scientific instruments, electrical and electronic equipment, aerospace equipment, luggage, food products, lumber, wood products and furniture, rubber and plastics products, primary metals, fabricated metal products, sporting goods, stone, glass, clay, and concrete products, textiles and apparel, transportation equipment

Natural Resources: Coal, oil shale, petroleum, natural gas, molybdenum, vanadium, zinc, uranium, gravel, sand, stone, rich soil, limestone, granite, marble, quartz, sandstone, copper, gold, silver, lead, clay, lime, gypsum, salt, pumice

Business: Wholesale and retail trade accounts for nearly six hundred thousand jobs and produces an estimated $42.2 billion per year. About two hundred thousand Colorado workers are employed in manufacturing. Colorado's employers include such giants as Martin-Marietta, Hewlett Packard, Johns Manville, Gates Rubber Company, and Honeywell. In recent years, many small high-tech companies have sprung up along the Front Range from Fort Collins to Colorado Springs, bringing many new jobs. Tourism adds about $4 billion to the economy every year.

Finance: Denver is the financial center of the Rocky Mountain states. Banking, insurance, real estate, and allied industries account for approximately one hundred thousand jobs in Colorado. The United States Mint in Denver produces 5 billion coins every year.

Communication: The *Rocky Mountain News*, published in Denver, is Colorado's oldest paper and is the major newspaper of the Rocky Mountain region. The *Denver Post* is another widely read daily. Other leading papers include the *Colorado Springs Gazette-Telegraph* and the *Pueblo Chieftain*. Colorado has about 165 radio stations and 15 television stations.

Transportation: Colorado has about 75,000 mi. (120,701 km) of roads, most of them paved. Interstate 70 is an east-west route across the middle of the state. Interstate 25 is a major north-south route across the state. Interstate 76 connects Denver with Interstate 80 near the Nebraska-Colorado border. The Eisenhower-Johnson Memorial Tunnel, which cuts through the mountains west of Denver at 11,000 ft. (3,353 m) above sea level, is the world's highest automobile tunnel. The road that climbs to the crest of 14,264-ft. (4,348-m) Mount Evans near Denver is the highest road in the United States. Colorado has about 3,500 mi. (5,633 km) of railroad track carrying passengers to ten cities and freight to many more. The 6.2-mi.- (10 -km-) long Moffat Tunnel, completed in 1927, is the nation's second-longest rail tunnel. Colorado has about 245 airports and is served by 21 airlines. Denver's Stapleton International Airport, the largest airport in the state, is the fifth-busiest airport in the United States.

SOCIAL AND CULTURAL LIFE

Museums: The Denver Museum of Natural History is one of the nation's largest natural-history museums. Of special interest are its large collection of minerals, its exhibits on prehistoric American peoples, and the daily programs offered at its Gate Planetarium. Other museums in Denver include the Denver Art Museum, which has an extensive collection of Native American art; the Train Art Museum and Gallery, which features European and Oriental works; the Museum of Western Art, one of the city's newest and finest museums; the Colorado State Museum, which traces the colorful history of Colorado Indians, miners, and settlers; the Black American West Museum and Heritage Center, which records the contributions of black cowboys in the development of the American West; and the Colorado Heritage Center, which is filled with the collection of the Colorado Historical Society. The Denver Children's Museum features many "hands on" exhibits. Other specialized museums in the Denver area include the Forney Transportation Museum, the Colorado Railroad Museum, the Denver Firefighters Museum, Buffalo Bill's Grave and Museum, and the Molly Brown House Museum. Also of interest in Denver are the Denver Zoo and the Denver Botanic Gardens.

Museums of note outside the Denver area include the University of Colorado Museum of Natural History and the Boulder Center for the Visual Arts, in Boulder; the Gold Mine Museum, in Central City; the Pro Rodeo Hall of Champions and the Colorado Springs Fine Arts Center, in Colorado Springs; and the Museum of Western Colorado, in Grand Junction. The Colorado State Historical Society operates museums in Fort Garland, Georgetown, Leadville, Platteville, Pueblo, Trinidad, and Montrose.

Libraries: Colorado has about 125 public libraries. The largest is the Denver Public Library, with 21 branches and more than one million bound volumes. The University of Colorado at Boulder has the state's largest university library.

Performing Arts: The Denver Symphony Orchestra performs classical music and children's concerts in Boettcher Concert Hall, the nation's oldest in-the-round concert hall. The Denver Center Theater Company, the Denver Center Cinema, Opera Colorado, and the Colorado Ballet are all featured at the Denver Center for

The open-air Red Rocks Amphitheater is surrounded by natural rock formations that provide excellent acoustics.

the Performing Arts, one of the nation's largest arts complexes. The Arvada Center for the Arts and Humanities books a variety of musical, dance, and theater events. The Elitch Theater Company, located in Elitch Gardens, is one of America's oldest summer-stock theaters. The Lowenstein Theater produces many children's plays.

The Aspen Music Festival, held every summer in Aspen, has received national acclaim. Summertime classical, rock, folk, and jazz concerts are held at the natural amphitheater at Red Rocks Park near Morrison. Summer classical concerts are also held in Vail and Boulder. Visitors flock to see summer performances at the Central City Opera House. The Colorado Shakespeare Festival is presented each summer in an outdoor theater on the campus of the University of Colorado at Boulder. The Creede Repertory Theater presents plays from the Victorian era.

Sports and Recreation: In professional sports, Denver is represented in the National Football League (NFL) by the Broncos, who play in 76,000-seat Mile High Stadium. The Denver Nuggets of the National Basketball Association (NBA) play in nearby McNichols Sports Arena. Fans of college football follow the teams of the University of Colorado at Boulder and the United States Air Force Academy at Colorado Springs. The annual Pikes Peak Hill Climb on July 4 is Colorado's major auto-racing event. Rodeos are very popular in Colorado. Some of the best-known rodeos in the state are the National Western Stock Show, the Greeley Spud Rodeo, and the rodeo held at the Colorado State Fair in Pueblo.

In the winter, Colorado is a skier's paradise. More than thirty ski areas and resorts attract skiers from all over the nation. During the rest of the year, Colorado provides sports enthusiasts with a huge variety of activities. Trout, walleyes, blue and silver bass, perch, and black crappies abound in Colorado's more than 11,000 mi. (17,703 km) of streams and 2,300 lakes. Hunters can find black bears, white-tailed and mule deer, pronghorn antelope, bighorn sheep, and mountain goats. Hiking, camping, white-water rafting, canoeing, horseback riding, golf, sailing, swimming, backpacking, and cycling are included on the nearly endless list of outdoor activities that can be enjoyed in the state. There is even a new "Colorado Trail," a 470-mi. (756-km) hiking pathway that runs from Denver to Durango. Built by volunteers, the trail crosses seven national forests, five major river systems, and six wilderness areas.

119

Historic Sites and Landmarks:

Bent's Fort, near La Junta, was perhaps the most important outpost along the northern branch of the famous Santa Fe Trail. Traders, trappers, Indians, and settlers met here during the early days of Colorado settlement. The original fort, completed in 1833, has been carefully reconstructed.

Central City Historic District, in Central City, includes the Teller House, site of the *Face on the Barroom Floor*. The district also features the Central Gold Mine and Museum, the restored Central City Opera House, and the St. James Methodist Church, said to be the oldest Protestant church in Colorado.

Chimney Rock Archaeological Site, in Archuleta County, is a national historic site where Pueblo ruins, kivas, and pit-house dwellings are arrayed on a mesa overlooking the Piedra River.

Durango & Silverton Narrow Gauge Railroad is one of the last operating narrow-gauge railroads in the nation. Built in 1882 to take silver out of the mines, it still carries passengers through the scenic San Juan Mountains between the two old mining towns of Durango and Silverton.

Fort Garland, in Costilla County, was once commanded by Kit Carson and was visited by General William Tecumseh Sherman in 1866. It has been restored and is maintained by the Colorado Historical Society.

Georgetown-Silver Plume Historic District, in Clear Creek County, includes such historically significant buildings as the Hotel De Paris, the Hamill House Museum, and the Alpine Hose #2 Fire House. One building, Maxwell House, has been cited as one of the ten outstanding Victorian houses in the United States.

Hovenweep National Monument, in Montezuma County along the Utah border, features six groups of prehistoric towers, pueblos, and cliff dwellings. Pueblo Indians inhabited the site from about A.D. 400 to 1300.

Larimer Square Historic District, in Denver, was the original business center of the city. Restored to look as it did in the nineteenth century, the district includes many specialized shops and fine restaurants.

Mesa Verde National Park, near Cortez, preserves the world's largest collection of ancient Indian cliff dwellings. Covering 52,000 acres (21,044 hectares), the site was inhabited by Pueblo people about a thousand years ago.

Telluride is a charming little town that has been designated a National Historic District. Its beautifully restored nineteenth-century buildings include the Opera House, City Hall, and the Sheridan Hotel. The town has been used as the backdrop for a number of motion pictures, including *The Unsinkable Molly Brown*, the story of one of Colorado's most famous residents.

Relics of the mining era such as these buildings (above) and this abandoned mine (right) can still be seen in Cripple Creek, where millions of dollars' worth of gold was produced in the 1890s.

Other Interesting Places to Visit:

Baca House and Bloom House, in Trinidad, are two restored nineteenth-century mansions that recall the age of the Colorado cattle barons. Baca House, which dates from 1869, once belonged to a wealthy Hispanic American merchant and farmer. Bloom House, which stands next door, is noted for its beautiful Victorian Rose Garden.

Colorado National Monument, near Grand Junction, affords views of such natural wonders as Red Canyon, Window Rock, the Coke Ovens, and 500-ft.- (152-m-) high Independence Rock.

Cripple Creek, in Teller County, is the site of what was once the largest known gold deposit in the world. The town's Imperial Hotel and Old Homestead date from the gold-rush days of the 1890s.

Dinosaur National Monument, in Moffat County, is a 325-sq.-mi. (842-km^2) park that has yielded remarkable dinosaur fossils. Scenic overlooks within the park offer spectacular views of the Green and Yampa rivers.

Florissant Fossil Beds National Monument, west of Colorado Springs, is a 6,000-acre (2,428-hectare) site that has yielded many well-preserved prehistoric fossils.

Four Corners Monument, in the southwest corner of the state, is the only spot in the United States where four states (Colorado, Utah, New Mexico, and Arizona) meet.

The Pikes Peak Incline Railway (left) takes visitors up to the top of Pikes Peak (above).

Garden of the Gods, near Colorado Springs, contains 700 acres (283 hectares) of unusually shaped sandstone rock formations.

Great Sand Dunes National Monument, in Alamosa and Saguache counties, contains the highest sand dunes in the United States. The dunes shift constantly, and their color seems to change with the angle of the sun.

Gunnison National Monument, near Montrose, features Black Canyon, the narrowest and deepest gorge in the United States.

Pikes Peak, near Colorado Springs, is Colorado's most-famous mountain. A toll road from Cascade climbs 7,309 ft. (2,228 m) to the 14,110-ft. (4,301-m) summit, and a cog railway runs to the top from Manitou Springs.

Left: The Royal Gorge of the Arkansas River
Above: The modernistic all-faith chapel at the United States Air Force Academy

Rocky Mountain National Park, in north-central Colorado, includes a 35-mi. (56-km) chain of huge mountain peaks, two hundred nature trails, forty-four lakes, and numerous waterfalls, mountain streams, and native alpine plants.

Royal Gorge of the Arkansas River, near Canon City, is a 1,200-ft.- (366-m-) deep chasm that is one of Colorado's most popular scenic attractions. The world's highest suspension bridge crosses the gorge, and an incline railway descends to its bottom.

State Capitol, in Denver, was modeled after the national capitol in Washington, D.C., and features a gold-plated dome. As befits the "Mile High City," the thirteenth step to the entrance of the building is exactly 1 mi. (1.6 km) above sea level.

United States Air Force Academy, near Colorado Springs, is the youngest of the nation's service academies. Opened in 1958, it is noted for its striking International Style architecture.

United States Mint, in Denver, produces five billion coins each year and is the nation's second-largest gold depository. Tours are given every weekday.

123

IMPORTANT DATES

c. A.D. 1 — The Basketmakers settle at Mesa Verde and take up farming

c. 400-750 — The Indians of Mesa Verde move from caves into pit houses and begin making clay pottery

c. 750-1100 — The Mesa Verde people begin grouping their dwellings into villages (pueblos) set on top of Mesa Verde

c. 1100-1300 — During what archaeologists call the Classic Pueblo Period, the culture of Mesa Verde's Pueblo people reaches its peak as the people move from their mesa-top homes to magnificently built cliff dwellings

c. 1300 — For unknown reasons, the Pueblo people of Mesa Verde begin abandoning their cliff towns

1541 — Francisco Vásquez de Coronado is thought to have crossed into southeastern Colorado on his way back to Mexico after a gold-seeking expedition

1598 — Juan de Oñate reaches the San Luis Valley during a gold-seeking expedition

1682 — Robert Cavelier, Sieur de La Salle, claims for France all of Colorado east of the Rocky Mountains

1706 — Juan de Ulibarri claims southeastern Colorado for Spain

1776 — Spanish missionaries Silvestre Escalante and Francisco Dominguez travel through western Colorado and name Mesa Verde

1803 — The Louisiana Purchase gives the United States most of eastern Colorado

1806 — Zebulon Pike explores Colorado for the United States and sights the peak that now bears his name

1819 — A treaty between the United States and Spain establishes the Arkansas River as the Louisiana Territory's southwestern border

1820 — Stephen H. Long leads the first recorded ascent of Pikes Peak

1833 — Bent's Fort, one of the most important trading posts in the American West, is completed

1842 — Jim Beckwourth establishes a settlement and trading post at Fort Pueblo

1848 — As part of the Treaty of Guadalupe Hidalgo ending the Mexican War, Mexico cedes western Colorado to the United States

1851—San Luis on the Culebra River becomes the first permanent white settlement in Colorado

1858—Gold is found where Cherry Creek flows into the South Platte River, sparking the "Pikes Peak or Bust" gold rush

1859—Prospectors strike gold at Idaho Springs, North Clear Creek, and other sites in Colorado; thousands of "Fifty-niners" flock to Colorado as the news of the Colorado gold rush spreads; Colorado's first newspaper, the *Rocky Mountain News*, is founded

1860—Gold is discovered at Leadville; Colorado's first public library opens in Denver

1861—Congress establishes the Colorado Territory; William Gilpin becomes the first territorial governor; Colorado City becomes the first territorial capital

1864—Some 150 Cheyenne Indians are killed in the Sand Creek Massacre

1867—Denver becomes the territorial capital

1870—The Denver Pacific Railroad connecting Denver with Cheyenne, Wyoming is completed; the Kansas Pacific line enters Colorado from the Missouri River; Union Colony is established at Greeley by Nathan Meeker

1875—Silver is discovered at Leadville

1876—Colorado becomes the thirty-eighth state

1879—During what becomes known as the Meeker Massacre, Ute Indians kill Indian Agent Nathan Meeker and eleven of his men; Ute chief Ouray attempts to resolve the differences between his people and the white settlers

1880—Ute chief Ouray dies

1881—The Utes are removed from western Colorado

1890—Passage of the Sherman Silver Act raises the price of silver and boosts Colorado's silver-mining industry

1891—Colorado's last big gold camp is opened at Cripple Creek

1893—A nationwide economic depression results in the collapse of the silver market; Colorado silver mines are shut down and many miners lose their jobs

1899—The state's first beet-sugar refinery is opened in Grand Junction

1906—The United States Mint at Denver produces its first coins; Mesa Verde National Park is established

The United States Mint in Denver began operating in 1906.

1914—Several women and children are killed when the National Guard confronts striking coal miners in what becomes known as the Ludlow Massacre

1915—Rocky Mountain National Park is established

1921—A disastrous flood in Pueblo kills more than a hundred people and causes $20 million in property damage

1927—The 6.4-mi.- (10.3-km-) long Moffat Tunnel is completed

1932-37—A disastrous drought and resulting "dust bowl" conditions across the Great Plains cause economic hardship for many Colorado farmers

1958—The United States Air Force Academy opens its campus near Colorado Springs

1959—The Colorado-Big Thompson Project is completed, providing irrigation for 720,000 acres (291,374 hectares) of farmland

1961—The National Center for Atmospheric Research is established at Boulder

1966—North American Aerospace Defense Command (NORAD) completes its underground center in Cheyenne Mountain

1973—The Eisenhower-Johnson Memorial Tunnel, the world's highest road tunnel, opens

1976—The Wayne N. Aspinall water-storage system is completed; a flood in Big Thompson Canyon near Loveland kills more than 135 people

1977 — The United States Solar Energy Research Institute opens near Denver

1983 — Federico Pena becomes Denver's first Hispanic mayor

1985 — The Frying Pan-Arkansas River Project is completed, bringing water from western Colorado to the eastern plains

IMPORTANT PEOPLE

Katharine Lee Bates (1859-1929), author and educator; her poem "America the Beautiful," which became a popular American anthem when later set to music, was inspired by her 1893 visit to Colorado

James Pierson (Jim) Beckwourth (1798-1867?), frontiersman and scout; lived with the Crow Indians (1826-37); ran trading posts in the Rocky Mountain area (1837-50); is credited with the founding and naming of Pueblo (1842)

William Bent (1809-1869), pioneer, fur trader; founded, with his brother Charles, Bent's Fort near present-day La Junta; became the most prominent Colorado citizen of his time; in the 1830s, he traded at the fort with the Cheyennes and hosted such notables as Kit Carson, Jim Bridger, and the armies of Kearny and Frémont; Bent County is named for him

Albert Bierstadt (1830-1902), landscape painter; traveled through the American West painting scenic panoramas; his works, especially *Storm in the Rocky Mountains* (1863), helped bring worldwide attention to Colorado's natural beauty

Black Kettle (?-1868), Cheyenne chief; his village was wiped out during the 1864 Sand Creek Massacre, a surprise attack that killed hundreds of warriors, women, and children, and that took place even though Black Kettle had agreed to an armistice with the American army; later, still trying to negotiate peace, he was killed when General George Custer raided his new camp (located in what is now Oklahoma)

Charles Boettcher (1852-1948), merchant, industrialist; pioneer Leadville merchant; organized the Colorado Portland Cement Company; was prominent in the development of the beet-sugar industry in the state

Frederick Gilmer Bonfils (1860-1933), newspaper publisher; became co-owner, with Harry H. Tammen, of the *Denver Post* in 1895; turned it into a sensationalized newspaper that eventually boasted the widest circulation in the Rocky Mountain states

JIM BECKWOURTH

ALBERT BIERSTADT

FREDERICK BONFILS

127

M. SCOTT CARPENTER

LON CHANEY

MARY CHASE

JACK DEMPSEY

Charles Franklin Brannan (1903-   ), born in Denver; lawyer and public official; attorney and administrator for the U.S. Department of Agriculture (1935-41), U.S. secretary of agriculture (1948-53)

Clara Brown (1803-1885), pioneer and nurse; slave who bought her freedom and joined the gold rush in 1859; later moved to Central City, where she turned her home into a hospital, church, and boardinghouse for poor miners

Margaret Tobin (Molly) Brown (1873-1932), Colorado mining-era pioneer; with her husband, James, made and lost several fortunes in Leadville mining; crashed New York, Newport, and European social circles, and survived the sinking of the *Titanic*; the story of her life was made into a Broadway musical, *The Unsinkable Molly Brown*

William Newton Byers (1831-1903), newspaperman; hauled a press and other equipment from Omaha to the Colorado goldfields, where he published and edited (1859-78) Colorado's first newspaper, the *Rocky Mountain News*

Malcolm Scott Carpenter (1925-   ), born in Boulder; U.S. Navy test pilot and astronaut; in 1962, in the Aurora 7 spacecraft, became the second American to orbit the Earth; retired in 1969 to enter private business

George Catlin (1796-1872), artist and author; traveled west in the 1830s to spend time among various Indian groups; painted their portraits and their way of life; in 1841 published a collection of sketches and notes that included one of the few sympathetic reports on the Comanches and Kiowas of southern Colorado

Lon Chaney (1883-1930), born in Colorado Springs; film actor; was called the "man of a thousand faces" because of his makeup skills and ability to change his physical appearance; best known for playing the title roles in *The Hunchback of Notre Dame* (1923) and *The Phantom of the Opera* (1925)

Mary Coyle Chase (1907-1981), born in Denver; playwright; best known for the 1945 Pulitzer Prizewinning play *Harvey*, about a gentle drunkard whose best friend is an invisible, six-foot-tall rabbit

William Harrison (Jack) Dempsey (1895-1983), born in Manassa; professional boxer; known as "The Manassa Mauler"; noted for his savage punches and an exciting ring style; world heavyweight boxing champion (1919-26)

John Denver (1943-   ), born Henry John Deutschendorf, Jr.; pop/folk singer, songwriter, and actor; changed his last name to Denver because of his love for the city; best known for such hit songs as "Rocky Mountain High," "Back Home Again," and "Thank God I'm a Country Boy"

John Elway (1960-   ), professional football player; quarterback who led the Denver Broncos to the Super Bowl in 1987 and 1988; voted Most Valuable Player in the National Football League (1987)

John Evans (1814-1897), physician, businessman, and public official; territorial governor of Colorado (1852-65); founded the Colorado Seminary, which later became the University of Denver (1864); in 1870 built the Denver Pacific Railroad, the first rail link between Denver and the East; Mount Evans is named for him

JOHN EVANS

Douglas Fairbanks (1883-1939), born Douglas Elton Ulman in Denver; film actor and producer; popular silent film star of such action-adventures as *The Mark of Zorro* (1920) and *The Thief of Bagdad* (1924); in 1920 founded the film production company United Artists with his wife, actress Mary Pickford, and actor Charlie Chaplin

Barney Ford (1824-1902), Colorado pioneer, hotelman, and social reformer; joined the Colorado gold rush in 1860 as a fugitive slave and stayed to found the luxurious Denver and Cheyenne Inter-Ocean Hotels; provided money, food, and jobs for runaway and freed slaves; set up Colorado's first adult education classes for blacks

DOUGLAS FAIRBANKS

Gene Fowler (1890-1960), born Eugene Devlan in Denver; newspaperman, author; best known for his biographies of popular personalities of the 1930s and 1940s; his *Timberline* (1933) is a scathing portrait of his former bosses at the *Denver Post*, Frederick Bonfils and Harry Tammen

Hamlin Garland (1860-1940), author; lived in Colorado and used it as the setting for ten books, including *They of the High Trails* (1916)

Horace Greeley (1811-1872), political and social reformer, newspaper editor, and founder of the *New York Tribune*; popularized the phrase "Go West, young man!"; his generally positive accounts of the Colorado goldfields, which he visited in 1859, encouraged many to make the trek to Colorado; helped found, with *Tribune* agricultural editor Nathan Meeker, a utopian community called the Union Colony; the colony's town, Greeley, was named for him

GENE FOWLER

Hannah Green (1932-   ), pen name of Joanne Goldenberg Greenberg; novelist and short-story writer; resides in Golden; best known for *I Never Promised You a Rose Garden*, the story of a teenage girl's experience in a psychiatric hospital, and the novel *The Far Side of Victory*

Meyer Guggenheim (1828-1905), industrialist, philanthropist; made a fortune in silver and lead from Leadville mines in the early 1880s; in 1888, believing that processing metals would be more profitable than mining them, built a smelting operation in Pueblo

HAMLIN GARLAND

WILLARD LIBBY

WILLIAM PALMER

ANNE PARRISH

FLORENCE SABIN

Gary Warren Hart (1937-   ), lawyer, politician; U.S. senator from Colorado (1975-87); campaigned for the Democratic presidential nomination in 1984 and 1988

Homer Lea (1876-1912), born in Denver; soldier of fortune; served as general and advisor to President Sun Yat-sen of China (1911); foresaw the danger of Japanese expansion in the Pacific

Willard Frank Libby (1908-1980), born in Grand Valley; chemist; received the 1960 Nobel Prize in chemistry for discovering the radiocarbon-dating method of determining the age of prehistoric plant and animal fossils

Stephen Harriman Long (1784-1864), army officer, engineer, explorer; provided the U.S. government with valuable information about the American West; in 1820, sighted and named Longs Peak in northern Colorado

Nathan Cook Meeker (1817-1879), journalist, social reformer; in 1870, founded the Union Colony at Greeley, a cooperative agricultural settlement; later served as Indian agent at the White River reservation; in what became known as the Meeker Massacre, was killed by the Utes after he tried to force them to create a planned agricultural community

David Halliday Moffat (1839-1911), banker, industrialist; promoted the railroad and mining industries in Colorado; served as president of Denver's First National Bank; Moffat Tunnel, one of the world's longest railroad tunnels, is named for him

Ouray (1820-1883), Ute chief; was respected by both his own people and white settlers for his efforts to promote peace between the two groups when Americans began exploiting Colorado for its minerals

William Jackson Palmer (1836-1909), soldier, railway executive, industrial promoter; helped develop the Colorado Territory; in 1871 founded the Denver and Rio Grande Railroad and established Colorado Springs as a planned community

Anne Parrish (1888-1957), born in Colorado Springs; author and illustrator; noted for such books as *The Perennial Bachelor* and *Floating Island*

Zebulon Montgomery Pike (1779-1813), army officer, explorer; sent to explore the Arkansas and Red rivers in 1806, he wound up in southeastern Colorado, where he sighted and made an unsuccessful attempt to scale the snow-covered peak that now bears his name

Florence Rena Sabin (1871-1953), born in Central City; scientist, public health pioneer; became the first woman elected to the National Academy of Sciences; her statue represents Colorado in Statuary Hall in the U.S. Capitol

Patricia Schroeder (1940-   ), politician; U.S. representative (1973-   ); first woman to serve on Congress's Armed Services Committee

Elizabeth McCourt Doe (Baby Doe) Tabor (1862-1935), second wife of mining millionaire H.A.W. Tabor; best known as the heroine of Douglas Moore's opera, *The Ballad of Baby Doe*, which recounts her last years as an impoverished widow

Horace Austin Warner Tabor (1830-1899), mining developer; joined the Pikes Peak gold rush in 1859 as a storekeeper; became wealthy when two of the many prospectors he had provided with food and cash found a silver lode in 1878; made a fortune from his Matchless Mine and other mining enterprises; spent lavish amounts of money on homes and on opera houses in Leadville and Denver; mayor and postmaster of Leadville (1878); lieutenant governor of Colorado (1879-83); lost his fortune when the silver market collapsed in 1893

Henry Moore Teller (1830-1914), public official; one of Colorado's first U.S. senators (1876-82, 1885-1909); U.S. secretary of the interior (1882-85); noted for the Teller Resolution (1898), which committed the United States to an independent Cuba; was a staunch supporter of the free coinage of silver

Lowell Jackson Thomas (1892-1981), news broadcaster, world traveler, author; grew up in Victor; best known for his nightly national radio news broadcasts (1930-76); narrated "Movietone News" (1935-52); author of more than fifty books, including *Good Evening Everybody* and *So Long Until Tomorrow*

Byron Raymond White (1917-   ), born in Fort Collins; lawyer, jurist; earned the nickname "Whizzer" as an outstanding football player at the University of Colorado; U.S. deputy attorney general (1961); associate justice of the U.S. Supreme Court (1962-   )

Paul Whiteman (1890-1967), born in Denver; musician and orchestra leader; popularized jazz in a symphonic format during the 1920s and 1930s; became known as the "King of Jazz"; first conductor to perform George Gershwin's *Rhapsody in Blue*

Ann Zwinger (1925-   ), author and illustrator; resides in Colorado Springs; her books, usually self-illustrated, focus on nature and natural history; works include *Beyond the Aspen Grove* and *A Desert County Near the Sea*

PATRICIA SCHROEDER

HORACE TABOR

PAUL WHITEMAN

GOVERNORS

John L. Routt	1876-1879	Oliver H. Shoup	1919-1923
Frederick W. Pitkin	1879-1883	William E. Sweet	1923-1925
James B. Grant	1883-1885	Clarence J. Morley	1925-1927
Benjamin H. Eaton	1885-1887	William H. Adams	1927-1933
Alva Adams	1887-1889	Edwin C. Johnson	1933-1937
Job A. Cooper	1889-1891	Ray H. Talbot	1937
John L. Routt	1891-1893	Teller Ammons	1937-1939
Davis H. Waite	1893-1895	Ralph L. Carr	1939-1943
Albert W. McIntire	1895-1897	John C. Vivian	1943-1947
Alva Adams	1897-1899	W. Lee Knous	1947-1949
Charles S. Thomas	1899-1901	Walter W. Johnson	1949-1951
James B. Orman	1901-1903	Dan Thornton	1951-1955
James H. Peabody	1903-1905	Edwin C. Johnson	1955-1957
Alva Adams	1905	Stephen L.R. McNichols	1957-1963
James H. Peabody	1905	John A. Love	1963-1973
Jesse F. McDonald	1905-1907	John D. Vanderhoof	1973-1975
Henry A. Buchtel	1907-1909	Richard D. Lamm	1975-1987
John F. Shafroth	1909-1913	Roy Romer	1987-
Elias M. Ammons	1913-1915		
George A. Carlson	1915-1917		
Julius C. Gunter	1917-1919		

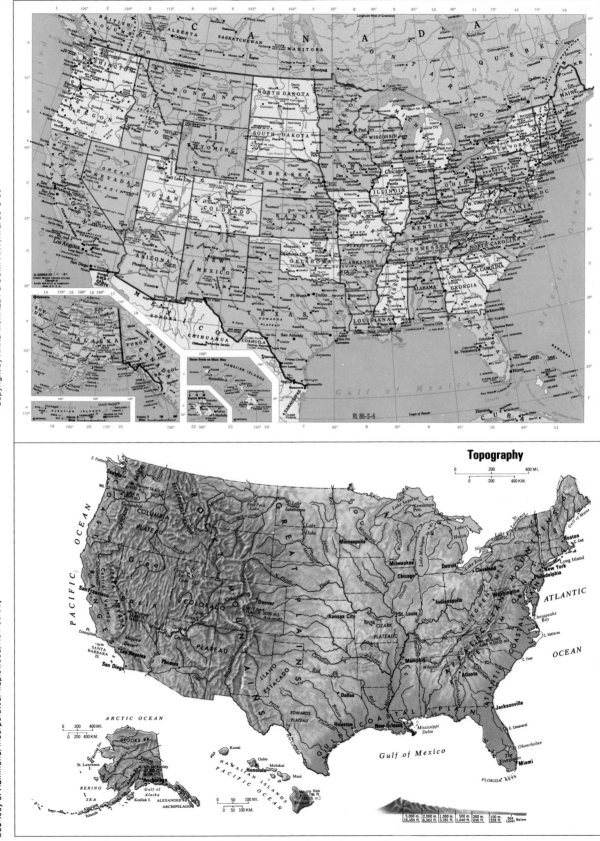

© Copyright by RAND McNALLY & COMPANY, R.L. 88-S-35

Courtesy of Hammond, Incorporated, Maplewood, New Jersey

Topography

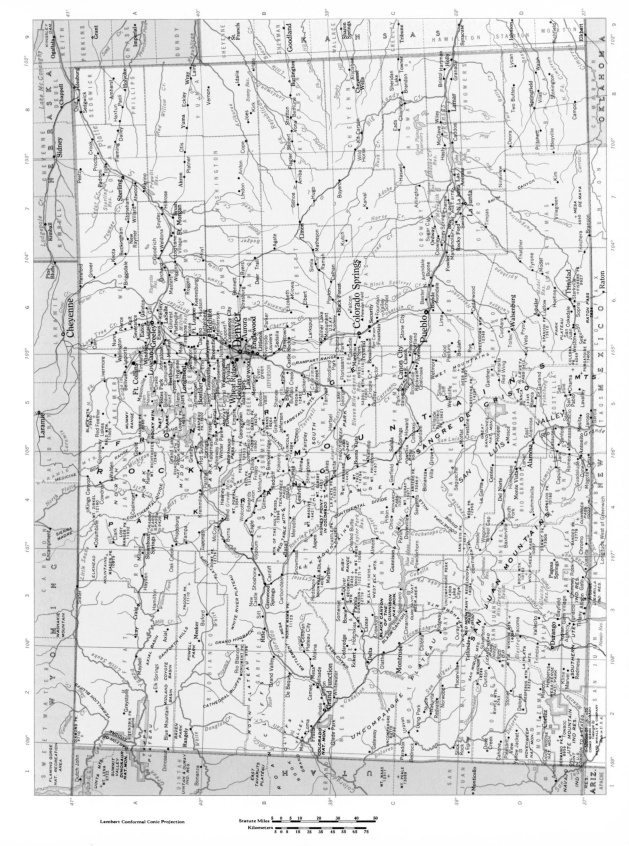

© Copyright by RAND McNALLY & COMPANY, R. L. 88-S-35

Lambert Conformal Conic Projection

Statute Miles
Kilometers

AVERAGE
YEARLY
PRECIPITATION

Centimeters		Inches
51 to 71		20 to 28
30 to 51		12 to 20
10 to 30		4 to 12

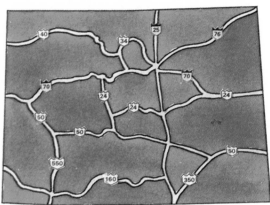

MAJOR HIGHWAYS

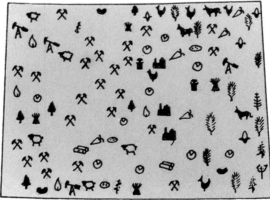

⬡ NATURAL GAS   🐔 POULTRY   🥔 POTATOES

🔥 OIL   🌾 BARLEY   ◐ VEGETABLES

⚒ MINING   SORGHUMS   🌳 FRUIT

🏭 MANUFACTURING   BEANS   ⊤ HAY

🥛 DAIRY   SUGAR BEETS   🐑 SHEEP

🐄 BEEF CATTLE   🌾 WHEAT   ⅄ BROOMCORN

📚 FOREST PRODUCTS   CORN   🌲 RYE

OATS

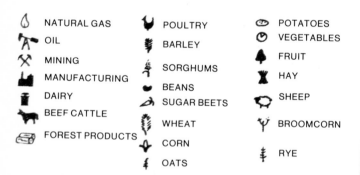

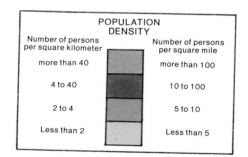

POPULATION
DENSITY

Number of persons per square kilometer		Number of persons per square mile
more than 40		more than 100
4 to 40		10 to 100
2 to 4		5 to 10
Less than 2		Less than 5

TOPOGRAPHY

Below Sea Level | 100 m. 328 ft. | 200 m. 656 ft. | 500 m. 1,640 ft. | 1,000 m. 3,281 ft. | 2,000 m. 6,562 ft. | 5,000 m. 16,404 ft.

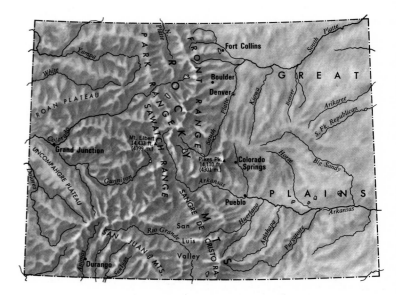

Courtesy of Hammond, Incorporated
Maplewood, New Jersey

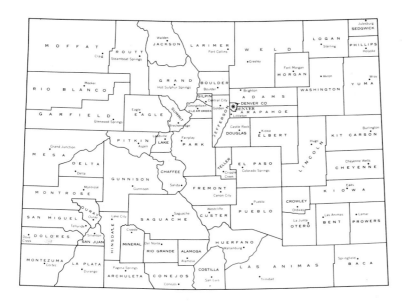

COUNTIES

Bear Creek in the Rocky Mountains

INDEX

Page numbers that appear in boldface type indicate illustrations

The business district of Denver as seen from the Civic Center

Picture Identifications
Front cover: Maroon Bells
Back cover: Downtown Denver
Pages 2-3: Delores Canyon
Page 6: Horseback riding near Ouray
Pages 8-9: The San Juan Mountains
Page 22: Montage of Colorado residents
Pages 26-27: Cliff Palace at Mesa Verde National Monument
Pages 34-35: An 1840 lithograph of an Indian buffalo hunt
Page 50: The Lost Horse Mill near Crystal City
Page 66: The state capitol in Denver
Pages 76-77: Fly fisherman standing in the Frying Pan River
Pages 88-89: Denver skyline
Page 108: Montage showing the state tree (Colorado blue spruce), the state bird (lark bunting), the state flower (Rocky Mountain columbine), the state animal (Rocky Mountain sheep), and the state flag

About the Author

Deborah Kent grew up in Little Falls, New Jersey, and received her bachelor's degree from Oberlin College. She obtained a master's degree in Social Work from the Smith College for Social Work, and a master's in Fine Arts from the University of Guanajuato in Mexico. She worked as a social worker in a New York City settlement house and taught disabled children in Mexico before she launched her career as a freelance writer. In addition to other books in the *America the Beautiful* series, she has written many novels for young adults.

Ms. Kent lives in Chicago with her husband and their daughter Janna.

Picture Acknowledgments

Root Resources: © Lia E. Munson: Front cover; © Kim G. Makower: Page 64;
© Kohout Productions: Pages 74, 108 (tree)
H. Armstrong Roberts: Page 113; © J. Gleiter: Pages 2-3; © D. Muench: Pages 4, 19 (middle);
© E. Cooper: Page 102 (right); © T. Ulrich: Page 108 (bird); © P. Buddle: Page 123 (left)
Nawrocki Stock Photo: © Steve Vidler: Pages 5, 54 (top), 66, 97, 105; © David Lissy: Pages 22
(top right, bottom left, bottom right, middle left), 88-89; © T.J. Florian: Page 69 (left); © Jayne
Kamin: Page 85 (right)
Odyssey Productions: © Walter Frerck: Page 6; © Robert Frerck: Pages 22 (top left), 73 (right)
Tom Stack & Associates: © Tom Algire Photography: Pages 8-9, 11; © Gene Marshall: Page 13
(bottom left); © Spencer Swanger: Pages 16, 37 (left), 71 (bottom right), 99 (top left, middle
right), 112; © Mary Clay: Page 19 (bottom right); © Gary K. Thompson: Page 20 (top right);
© Larry Brock: Page 20 (bottom left); © Stewart M. Green: Page 29 (bottom right); © Doug Lee:
Pages 85 (left), 103; © Brian Parker: Pages 86, 87, 123 (right); © Tom Stack: Page 91; © Perry
Conway: Page 92; © Tom E. Myers: Page 94; © Wendy Shattil/Robert Rozinski: Pages 99 (top
right), 108 (sheep); © Wilson Goodrich: Page 104
M.L. Dembinsky, Jr.: © Gary C. Baker: Page 12; © Jean Reuther: Page 19 (top right); © Carl R.
Sams II: Page 20 (top left)
Marilyn Gartman Agency: © Wilson Goodrich: Pages 13 (top left, top right, bottom right), 21
(right), 75, 110, 114, 138; © Wally Hampton: Page 17
Superstock International: Page 14; © Three Lions: Pages 26-27, 29 (left), 96 (both photos), 141
© **Jerry Hennen:** Page 15 (top left)
Historical Pictures Service Inc., Chicago: Pages 31, 37 (right), 52, 53; © D. Wagner: Page 15
(bottom left, right)
© **Chip & Rosa Maria Peterson:** Pages 18 (both photos), 73 (left)
Photri: Page 119; © M. Long: Page 19 (top left)
© **Reinhard Brucker:** Pages 19 (bottom left), 20 (bottom right), 83 (right), 122 (top)
EKM Nepenthe: © Robert L. Potts: Pages 21 (left), 108 (columbine)
Third Coast Stock Source: © John Nienhuis: Pages 22 (center), 71 (top right)
© **Virginia Grimes:** Pages 22 (middle right), 43 (right)
© **James R. Rowan:** Pages 22 (bottom center), 38 (left)
R/C Photo Agency: © Richard L. Capps: Page 29 (top right); © Janet Schleeter: Page 38 (right);
© Betty Kubis: Pages 69 (right), 106 (left); © J.M. Halama: Page 99 (bottom left, bottom right);
© Earl L. Kubis: Pages 101, 106 (right); © Frank Milne: Page 121 (both photos)
The Bettmann Archive, Inc.: Pages 34-35, 40 (left), 41, 55, 82 (left), 127 (Beckwourth,
Bierstadt), 128 (Chaney, Dempsey), 129 (Fairbanks, Garland), 130 (Palmer), 131 (Tabor)
Colorado Historical Society: Pages 40 (right), 42, 43 (left), 45 (all photos), 46, 49, 56, 57, 59,
60, 62
© **Joseph A. DiChello, Jr.:** Page 50
Journalism Services: © Rich Clark: Page 54 (bottom), 76-77; © Dirk Gallian: Page 71 (left);
© Gregory Murphey: Back cover
Cameramann International, Ltd.: Pages 81, 84, 116, 126
The Brooklyn Museum: Page 82 (right)
Wide World Photos: Pages 83 (left), 127 (Bonfils), 128 (Carpenter, Chase), 129 (Evans,
Fowler), 130 (Libby, Parrish, Sabin), 131 (Schroeder, Whiteman)
© **Bob & Ira Spring:** Page 102 (left)
© **Joan Dunlop:** Page 122 (bottom)
Len W. Meents: Maps on pages 91, 94, 101, 103, 136
Courtesy Flag Research Center, Winchester, Massachusetts 01890: Flag on Page 108

J978.8   Kent, Deborah.
              America the Beautiful: Colorado.

      12 PEACHTREE
ATLANTA FULTON PUBLIC LIBRARY

R00440 64711   DEC 1 7 1990